THE
OLIVET DISCOURSE

What the Lord Jesus Said About His Second Coming

DR. CHARLIE FOUCHÉ

THE
OLIVET DISCOURSE

What the Lord Jesus Said About His Second Coming

DR. CHARLIE FOUCHÉ

ISBN# 978-1-61119-15-1

Printed in the United States of America.

Printed by Calvary Publishing
A Ministry of Parker Memorial Baptist Church
1902 East Cavanaugh Road
Lansing, Michigan 48910
www.CalvaryPublishing.org

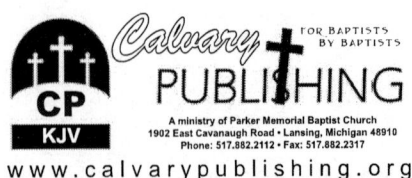

Calvary PUBLISHING
FOR BAPTISTS BY BAPTISTS
CP KJV
A ministry of Parker Memorial Baptist Church
1902 East Cavanaugh Road • Lansing, Michigan 48910
Phone: 517.882.2112 • Fax: 517.882.2317
www.calvarypublishing.org

CONTENTS

CHAPTER ONE

THE SIGNS OF THE TIMES

MATTHEW 24:1-4

INTRODUCTION

Many people today are interested in the future. What does the future hold? The Olivet Discourse in **Matthew 24-25** is THE most important sermon ever preached on the subject of prophecy. It is important because it came from the Lord Jesus Christ Himself. When looking at any passage in the Word of God, we must remember the context. Our Lord had just given a scathing rebuke to the Jewish leaders of His day in **Matthew 23**. He told them that the Jewish people had killed all the prophets that He had sent them (**Matthew 23:34-35**); He told them that they had rejected Him as their long-awaited and prophesied Messiah (**Matthew 23:37**); and He had just pronounced destruction on the pride of Jewish life—the Temple in Jerusalem (**Matthew 23:38**). Our Lord Jesus leaves the Temple for the last time. He leaves through the Beautiful Gate, and crosses the Brook Kidron. It was the same path His father King David had taken centuries before on the night he was also rejected as King of Israel. (**2 Samuel 15:23**) Like Lot's wife (**Genesis 19:26**), the disciples looked over their shoulders at the Temple as they made their ascent on the Mount of Olives east of David's city. How could all that the Lord spoke happen? They wanted to know the future of the Nation of Israel.

> **And Jesus went out, and departed from the temple: and his disciples came to *him* for to shew him the buildings of the temple.**
> [**Matthew 24:1**]

Departed

That was the final day the Lord Jesus Christ ever stepped Foot in the Jewish Temple. The Jewish Messiah departs, never to return to that building. This reminds us of the Shekinah Glory of God departing of the Temple in the Old Testament. (**Ezekiel 10:18**) With Jehovah gone from the Jewish religion, it became a mere hollow, empty ritual. Having rejected its Messiah, all that remained for the Jewish religion and Temple was destruction. The Lord Jesus will not enter a Jewish Temple again until He returns in great power and glory to reign as God-King in the Millennial Kingdom.

Temple

The Olivet Discourse was prompted by the disciples' pride in the Temple. The Jewish mindset was that the LORD God was with the nation of Israel because of the presence of the Temple. But just because the Jewish nation had a Temple, does not mean that it had the presence of God. Just before the nation went into exile in Babylon, the prophet Jeremiah warned the nation not to trust in the Temple building, but rather told Israel that she should look to the One Who dwelt in the Temple. **Jeremiah 7:4** The Temple at the time of the disciples was originally built by the Jewish exiles that returned to the Promised Land during the reign of Cyrus of Persia. (**Ezra 1:1-3**) King Herod began a beautification and expansion project on this Temple in 20 BC. By the time of the Lord Jesus, this project had been under construction for almost fifty years. (**John 2:20**) This expansion was finally completed in AD 67. Three years later, the Roman army came to Jerusalem and destroyed the magnificent Jewish Temple. People had come from all over the world to Jerusalem to view and visit the Temple. The complex itself covered thirty-five acres of real estate in downtown Jerusalem. The disciples tried to impress the Lord Jesus with the opulence and magnificence of the Temple. After all, it was GOD'S House.

And Jesus said unto them, See ye not all these things? verily I say unto you, There shall not be left here one stone upon another, that shall not be thrown down.

[Matthew 24:2]

These things

The Lord Jesus was NOT impressed! He had wept over the land, the city and the Temple. **Luke 19:41** He KNEW what would happen to His holy city.

Stone

Some of these magnificent stones were twenty-four feet long, and weighed several tons each. These massive stones at the base of the Temple had been cut in the quarries to exact specifications so that they would fit like a jigsaw puzzle when they were carried to the Temple Mount.

Thrown down

The destruction of the Temple at Gentile hands was prophesied as early as **Psalm 79:1**. That destruction was called for in the Providence of Almighty God. In AD 67, war with Rome broke out. General Titus, the Roman commander, issued an order not to destroy the Jewish Temple. But God had already decreed that it would be destroyed. A

Roman soldier, perhaps not knowing of the order, started a fire. As the gold melted in the heat of the flames, Roman soldiers took huge crowbars and forced each stone out of place looking for melted gold between the cracks of the rocks. This prophecy was fulfilled in AD 70 just exactly as the Lord Jesus had predicted. Literally, not one stone had been left upon another!

> **And as he sat upon the mount of Olives, the disciples came unto him privately, saying, Tell us, when shall these things be? and what *shall be* the sign of thy coming, and of the end of the world?**
> **[Matthew 24:3]**

He sat upon the Mount of Olives

The Mount of Olives was an important place in Jewish history and prophecy. From it, the Lord Jesus gave the greatest sermon on the Second Coming that was ever preached. **Mark 13:3.** It was a place where the Lord Jesus sought refuge at night, as He slept in the open air. **John 8:1** On the night of His betrayal, it was the place where the Lord Jesus led His disciples, and prayed in agony to the Father beneath the moonbeams as they shone through the olive trees. **Luke 22:39** But most importantly, it was the prophesied place where the Jewish Messiah would come to usher in His Millennial Kingdom. It was prophesied so in the Old Testament, **Zechari-**

ah 14:4 as well as in the New Testament. **Acts 1:12** According to the Word of God, the Mount of Olives will be the geographic place where the Lord Jesus touches when He returns in His Glory to set up His Thousand-Year Reign.

The disciples asked the Lord Jesus three distinct questions about His prophecy. 1) When shall these things be? That is, when will the destruction He spoke of in **Matthew 23:37-39** take place? That question is not answered in the Gospel of Matthew. The answer is recorded in **Luke 21:20-24.**

> **And when ye shall see Jerusalem compassed with armies, then know that the desolation thereof is nigh. Then let them which are in Judaea flee to the mountains; and let them which are in the midst of it depart out; and let not them that are in the countries enter thereinto. For these be the days of vengeance, that all things which are written may be fulfilled. But woe unto them that are with child, and to them that give suck, in those days! for there shall be great distress in the land, and wrath upon this people. And they shall fall by the edge of the sword, and shall be led away captive into all nations: and Jerusalem shall be trodden down of the Gentiles, until the times of the Gentiles be fulfilled.**

2) What shall be the sign of thy coming? The Lord Jesus answers this in **Matthew 24:29-44.** 3)

What shall be the sign of thy coming, and of the end of the world? The Lord Jesus answers this question in **Matthew 24:4-8.**

The sign

The Olivet Discourse is a distinctly Jewish sermon, and a distinctively Jewish prophecy. It has nothing to do with the Church. This is seen in the language the Lord Jesus uses throughout the sermon. Here, the disciples are asking for signs. We know from **1 Corinthians 1:22; Luke 11:29** and **John 6:30** that signs are for the Jewish people, NOT the church. The Rapture of the church was still a mystery hidden in the secret councils of God. The disciples did NOT know about the Rapture, and did not know to ask about it. The doctrine of the Rapture was not revealed until a converted Jewish Pharisee named Saul of Tarsus received That Revelation in **1 Thessalonians 4:13-18.**

Of thy coming

The Second Coming of the Lord Jesus to Earth will be a visible and glorious event. His Feet will touch Planet Earth on top of the Mount of Olives, the place from which He was speaking to the disciples, and the place from which this magnificent sermon was preached. **Zechariah 14:4; Acts 1:11-12** The Bible teaches a visible, glorious return of the

Lord Jesus to Earth. **Revelation 1:7** The Word of God knows nothing of a secret return of the Messiah that has already taken place. (Of course, we are taking for granted that the reader will understand the difference between the Rapture of the Church and the Second Coming of Christ.)

And of the end of the world

This word may also be translated "age," as it is in other places in the New Testament. **2 Corinthians 4:4** tells us that Satan is the God of this world/age/political and economic system. These terms can be used interchangeably. The disciples were concerned about the end of Satan's kingdom, and the beginning of the Messiah's Prophesied Millennial Kingdom. They knew the Old Testament teaching of the Day of the Lord, which would end Satan's rule on Earth and begin the Promised Millennial Reign of the Messiah. The Millennial Kingdom of the Messiah on Earth was the Old Testament "blessed hope" of the Hebrew people. It is with this Old Testament, Jewish mindset that the disciples ask these three questions.

> **And Jesus answered and said unto them, Take heed that no man deceive you.**
>
> [**Matthew 24:4**]

Verses 4-8 describe the first half of the seven-year Tribulation Period. It is also known as the Seventieth Week of **Daniel 9:24-27**. The first half of these final seven years before the Coming of the Lord is the time in which the first seven seals of **Revelation 6** come upon the Earth. The Old Testament prophesies of this seven-year Tribulation Period. **Jeremiah 30:4-9; Joel 2:1-17; Hosea 5:14; Ezekiel 30:4-9; Daniel 12:1; Micah 7:1-7; Habakkuk 3:16**

Take heed that no man

The Lord Jesus focuses on the end-time false messianic movements. We have seen our share of them in the twentieth and twenty-first centuries. We have seen charismatic individuals cross the stage of world history, fooling the masses, and gathering followings of millions bent on destruction. We have seen men like Adolph Hitler, Nikolai Lenin, Chairman Mao, Karl Marx, Idi Amin come, destroy, and go. The West has abandoned its Judeo-Christian heritage and opened a vacuum for satanic cults, Eastern religions, liberal Christendom, and the latest threat, Islam. After the Rapture, the devil's messiah will deceive the entire world into following him.

Deceive you

Religious deception will be a mark of the last days. Satan has been deceiving man since the Garden of Eden, but he will intensify his efforts during the last days because he will know that he has a little time left to drag every human soul into hell before the Second Coming of Christ. **Revelation 12:12** Scripture warns the believer of the end times of the religious deception that will mark the final days. **2 Thessalonians 2:3; Revelation 12:9**

> **For many shall come in my name, saying, I am Christ; and shall deceive many.**
>
>   [**Matthew 24:5**]

Many shall come in my name, saying, I am Christ

This statement of the Lord Jesus corresponds to the first seal of **Revelation 6:1-2**. This is the arrival of THE Antichrist, and the beginning of the seven-year Tribulation Period. The rider on a white horse comes with a bow, but no arrow. In other words, he comes with a show of might, but he comes in peace. According to **Daniel 9:27**, the Antichrist will begin the Tribulation Period by signing a seven-year peace treaty with the nation of Israel. The language here also shows that this coming conqueror will claim to be God. The words **I AM** is the Old Testament Name of Jehovah God of Israel. **Exodus 3:14** When the Lord Jesus claimed this Divine Name for Himself, the Jewish leaders understood His claim to be Jehovah God of the Old Testament, and sought to stone Him for blasphemy. **John 8:58-59** This also should put to rest the liberal misconception that the Lord Jesus never claimed to be God. He most certainly did, and the Jewish religious leaders not only understood His claim, they tried to stone Him to death for making Himself equal with God. **John 5:18** With today's New Age movement, and other humanistic religions, many are claiming divinity for themselves. It is the same old lie with which the father of lies began deceiving man in the Garden of Eden. **Ye shall be as gods. Genesis 3:5** It was the first sin in the universe, hatched within the heart of Lucifer. **Isaiah 14:13-14** Satan has always wanted to be God, and has passed that idea along to man. The final deception will be the antichrist claiming to be God's Messiah. He will be Satan's superhuman, who will deceive the world into thinking he is the Promised Messiah. **2 Thessalonians 2:4**

Shall deceive many

The Antichrist will use false miracles to deceive the masses during the Great Tribulation Period. **Revelation 13:11-14** This is why believers in the church age must know the Word of God. Satan's men will be able to work false miracles in order to make it appear they have heavenly power. Their "power" actually comes from hell. Believers are instructed in the Word of God to test the spirits of those who claim to be from God. **1 John 4:1-3** Not every preacher or prophet that claims he is from God is REALLY from God. You can tell a false spirit by what it says about the Lord Jesus Christ. It is the message that is important, not the miracles. The Lord Jesus warned of such imposters in the last days. **Matthew 7:15**

> **And ye shall hear of wars and rumours of wars: see that ye be not troubled: for all *these things* must come to pass, but the end is not yet.**
> **[Matthew 24:6]**

Ye shall hear of wars and rumours of wars

This corresponds to the second seal of **Revelation 6:3-4**. Wars have plagued mankind since the beginning of recorded human history. The Bible tells us of the first world war in **Genesis 14.** Mankind will never solve the problem of war. The League of Nations did not solve this problem after World War I. The United Nations has not solved the problem of war. This world will never have peace until the Prince of Peace reigns in the perfect peace of the Millennial Kingdom. **Isaiah 9:6**

> **For nation shall rise against nation, and kingdom against kingdom: and there shall be famines, and pestilences, and earthquakes, in divers places.**
> **[Matthew 24:7]**

Nation shall rise against nation

The Greek word for nations here is *ethnos*. This word is used in the New Testament for the term "race." During the final estate of the redeemed, all prejudice and racism will be healed. **Revelation 22:2** The redeemed will understand that in Christ, there is no racial, social, economic, or gender distinctions. **Galatians 3:28; Colossians 3:11** The only color that will matter is Red, which is the Blood of Christ that has been applied to the human soul.

There shall be famines

This corresponds to the third seal of **Revelation 6:5-8**. Famines are so common that they rarely get any attention nowadays. More than three-quarters of the world goes to bed hungry, with no hope of a better day tomorrow. Famine is always a side-effect of war, which will be an ongoing exercise in the Tribulation Period.

Pestilences

We have seen the new "super virus" come on the scene. We have been giving our children so many antibiotics that a new strain of "super virus" has arisen that is non-responsive to the medicines known to man. The Ebola virus is a new virus that is sweeping the world with no end in sight. There are strains that will kill a human within twenty-four hours of infection. The Bubonic Plague, or "Black Death," that plagued Europe in the fourteenth and fifteenth centuries is making a comeback. Twenty-five years ago, nobody had heard of the HIV virus or AIDS. This dreaded disease is the result of man's promiscuity and disregard for the natural laws of God. Mankind cannot shake his fist in the face of Almighty God without facing the consequences. Sin ALWAYS carries its own penalty, and mankind is reaping what he has sown. **Galatians 6:7-8**

Earthquakes

Earthquakes corresponds to the sixth seal of **Revelation 6:12-14**. Earthquakes are increasing in frequency and intensity. The world is waiting for "The Big One" that will give the state of California a new West Coastline. We are now discovering that many places where man has built cities are in the middle of huge fault lines. Earthquakes could affect and afflict several millions of people in these metropolitan areas. The Great Rift Valley runs from Lake Victoria in Africa through the city of Jerusalem on its way into Turkey. We can now see that the great earthquake prophesied in the sixth seal is a scientific reality waiting to happen.

All these *are* the beginning of sorrows.
[**Matthew 24:8**]

All these are the beginning

The characteristics or happenings of the first half of the Tribulation Period refer to what the Lord Jesus said in **verses 5-7.**

Sorrows

This is literally "birth pangs." The Old Testament pictures a woman in travail (birth pangs) as a picture of the intensity of the Great Tribulation Period. **Isaiah 13:6-11; Isaiah 26:17; Isaiah 66:7; Hosea 13:13; Micah 4:9; Revelation 12:2. Jeremiah 30:6-7** refers to the travail at the beginning of Jacob's Trouble. In **1 Thessalonians 5:3** it shows this time of intense travail will come immediately after the Rapture of the church, which is when the Tribulation Period will begin.

> **Then shall they deliver you up to be afflicted, and shall kill you: and ye shall be hated of all nations for my name's sake.**
> **[Matthew 24:9]**

Then

This does not mean AFTER these things happen. It means DURING the times of sorrows or birth pangs. That is, during the first half of the Tribulation Period.

Deliver you up to be afflicted

This corresponds to the fourth and fifth seals of **Revelation 6:7-11**. It will be a time of great martyrdom. Those who accept the Gospel of the Kingdom will be hunted down and killed by the Antichrist. (The Gospel of the Kingdom is the Good News that the Promised, Prophesied Messianic Kingdom of the Old Testament is Coming! This is NOT the same as the Gospel of the Grace of the Lord Jesus Christ, which is the Good News of the Death, Burial and Resurrection of Christ for human sins. **1 Corinthians 15:3-4** More will be said about this in **verse 14**.) Tens of thousands and possibly hundreds of thousands will be killed during the first half of the Tribulation for believing in the Coming King. Jewish followers of the Coming Messiah will be hunted down, persecuted, starved, fired from jobs, shunned by society and killed for their beliefs. The Lord Jesus promised all of His followers that He has overcome the tribulation we will face in this world, and He will deliver His followers—either in life or in death. **John 16:33; Revelation 1:9**

Hated of all nations

Anti-Semitism has been around on Earth since the call of Abraham. We have seen many instances of attempted extermination of the Jewish people. There was the Egyptian attempt to destroy all Jewish boys. **Exodus 1:15-22** There was the Persian attempt to eliminate the Jews under Haman. **Esther 3** There was the Spanish Inquisition; the Russian pogroms; and most recently the German Nazi holocaust. The twentieth and twenty-first centuries have produced no better attitude of the world toward the Jewish people. We have now seen the new weapon of terror unleashed upon the Jews in the Holy Land. There is a new breed of suicide bomber that will gladly give his life to kill Jews, for he thinks he will get an eternal reward for doing so. Yet the worst wave of anti-Semitism is still to come. The Antichrist will make Adolph Hitler look like a choirboy. He will attempt—and almost succeed—to complete Hitler's "Final Solution." The scope of his fury will be anyone who refuses to worship him, or who will harbor or help a Jew. This worldwide dragnet will begin in the first half of the Tribulation Period.

> And then shall many be offended, and shall betray one another, and shall hate one another.
> [Matthew 24:10]

Many will be offended

This refers to mere professors. There are many today who can speak "churchese." They know all the right things to say when around believers, but they have never really been born again. During the

Tribulation, those who were mere professors, but not possessors of Eternal Life, will have missed the Rapture. No doubt, for the first few weeks they will continue their church attendance as usual. Many will think they are believers. Their lives after the Rapture will show that they are not.

Betray

There have always been those who have betrayed others. The Lord Jesus, Who was preaching this sermon, knew well what it was like to be betrayed by one of His trusted friends. Chairman Mao used this tactic to brainwash an entire nation of Chinese children. He used the public school system as a tool to brainwash an entire generation of young communists to betray their parents, and turn them in to the government for their belief in Christ. During the Tribulation, many will betray neighbours, friends, and family members in hopes of some kind of immunity and favoritism by showing loyalty to the Antichrist.

> **And many false prophets shall rise, and shall deceive many.**
>
> **[Matthew 24:11]**

Many false prophets shall rise

The Lord Jesus warned of false prophets. **Mat-**

thew 24:24; Mark 13:22 The rise of many false prophets preaching "another gospel" was foretold throughout the Word of God as a sign of the last days. **1 Timothy 4:2; 2 Timothy 3; 2 Timothy 4:3; 1 John 4:1** There will be many that run through this Earth once the church has been raptured. However, God will NOT leave Himself without a witness. He will raise up two great witnesses (**Revelation 11**) who will work with 144,000 Jewish evangelists (**Revelation 7 and Revelation 14**). Millions will be saved after the Rapture during the ministry of those believers that the Lord will raise to witness to the Coming King.

> **And because iniquity shall abound, the love of many shall wax cold.**
>
> [**Matthew 24:12**]

Iniquity

This is elsewhere also translated "lawlessness." It is a condition of total anarchy, where there is no law. The world will have NO authority except its own mind and will. It will be just like in the time of Judges. **Judges 21:25** The Lawless One will take control of the world, and will institute his law in his rule. **2 Thessalonians 2:8**

Love of many shall wax cold

This shows the attitude of the world today.

Abortion abounds today. The fact that mothers can kill their own children with no remorse shows that the love of many is already waxing cold. It is a sign of the end times about which Paul wrote to Timothy. **2 Timothy 3:3** When the Antichrist announces his reign, the self-absorbed world will be more interested in self-preservation than love. Selfishness is the exact opposite of love.

> **But he that shall endure unto the end, the same shall be saved.**
>   [**Matthew 24:13**]

Endure unto the end

This has nothing to do with a Christian's salvation. The Christian is not to endure his salvation. He is to ENJOY his salvation. This has reference to enduring to the end of the seven-year Tribulation Period. Many Jews will NOT endure. Two out of every three Jews entering the Tribulation Period will be hunted down and killed ruthlessly by the administration of the Antichrist. Many Jews and Gentiles will become believers in the Coming Messiah-King during the Tribulation Period. But many of those will become the martyrs of **Revelation 7:9-17**. This is a reminder from the Lord Jesus that He will keep His Old Testament promises to the nation of Israel. He promised to keep a remnant until His

Coming, despite appearances to the contrary, and the faithlessness of the nation. **Isaiah 4:3; Matthew 10:22; Revelation 7:3**

The same shall be saved

All Jews who survive the Tribulation Period and witness the coming of the Messiah-King will be **saved**. They will enter the Millennial Kingdom and experience the promises to Israel of the Old Testament. Saved points back to the Old Testament prophecy of **Jeremiah 30:7**, which says,

> **Alas! for that day *is* great, so that none *is* like it: it *is* even the time of Jacob's trouble; but he shall be saved out of it.**

The salvation here refers to the deliverance of the Messiah-King to the Jewish people as He sets up His Millennial Kingdom. Israel will be saved (or delivered) out of the Great Tribulation Period. All Israel will be saved in that day, as the Scriptures promise. **Isaiah 66:8; Romans 11:26**

> **And this gospel of the kingdom shall be preached in all the world for a witness unto all nations; and then shall the end come.**
>
> **[Matthew 24:14]**

The Gospel of the Kingdom

The Bible teaches that there is only one way to salvation—through faith in the shed Blood of the Lord Jesus Christ on the Cross of Calvary. But the Bible also teaches that there are different gospels. The Gospel unto salvation is the Death, Burial and Resurrection of the Lord Jesus Christ. **1 Corinthians 15:3-4** There are also false gospels out there, which are NOT gospels at all. **Galatians 1:7** This Gospel of the Kingdom is the Good News that the prophecies of the Messiah's Kingdom are about to be fulfilled on planet Earth. This was the same Gospel that was preached at the beginning of the Lord Jesus' ministry. John Baptist preached the Gospel of the Kingdom when he told the nation of Israel that **the kingdom of heaven** is at hand. **Matthew 3:2** It is the same Gospel Message that the Lord Jesus Himself preached at the beginning of His public ministry to the nation of Israel. **Matthew 4:17; Mark 1:14** In the Old Testament, God Himself was rejected as King by the nation of Israel. **1 Samuel 8:7** In the Gospels, the nation of Israel rejected its Messiah as King, and gave Him a Cross instead of a Crown. **John 19:15** In the Book of Acts, the nation of Israel rejected the Holy Spirit's ministry to the witness of the Lord Jesus Christ. Israel's spiritual leaders persecuted and killed the early church as it gave witness that the Lord Jesus was the Promised

Messiah-King. **Acts 7:54-60** The preaching of the Gospel of the Kingdom ceased. From thenceforth, the Lord has seen fit to reveal the mystery of the church to Paul, and the living Body of Christ was instituted to spread the Gospel of Jesus Christ to a lost and dying world. **Ephesians 1:4-10** When the church age has run its course—when it is raptured from Planet Earth—144,000 Jewish evangelists will preach the Gospel of the Kingdom once again. **Revelation 7** They will spread upon the Earth the Good News that the Messiah-King is coming from Heaven to deliver His people.

Shall be preached in all the world

In the Tribulation Period, God will make sure that His Message of the Coming Messiah-King will be spread throughout the entire world. **Romans 10:18** He will use the 144,000 Jewish evangelists, but He will also use the angelic beings to proclaim the Gospel of the Coming King. **Revelation 14:6** There is no need for the liberal concern about people in the south-sea islands who may have never heard the Gospel. In the final days, the Lord God Himself will make sure all peoples, nations, languages, and ethnic groups have an opportunity to hear the Gospel. Until then, what are WE doing to share the Gospel?

Nations

This is the Greek word *ethnos*, which literally means "all peoples." The Lord Jesus came the first time for ALL people. **Galatians 3:28** He is coming back for the same **whosoever will** of Planet Earth. **Revelation 22:17** The 144,000 will spread the Gospel of the Kingdom to all the Earth, and people from every nation, tongue, strata of society, color, religion and climate will have the opportunity to believe in the Coming Messiah-King.

CHAPTER TWO

THE GREAT TRIBULATION BEGINS

MATTHEW 24:15-31

When ye therefore shall see the abomination of desolation, spoken of by Daniel the prophet, stand in the holy place, (whoso readeth, let him understand:)

[Matthew 24:15]

The Olivet Discourse in THE most important prophetic sermon ever preached. What makes it of such significance is that it came from the Lips of the Lord Jesus Christ Himself. It is the skeleton which supports ALL other Biblical prophecy. The midpoint of the Tribulation Period is extremely important to the understanding of all Biblical prophecy. An event prophesied in **Daniel 9:24-27** begins the start of the Seventieth Prophetic Week. That will be the signing of a seven-year peace treaty between the Antichrist and the nation of Israel. **2 Thessalonians 2:1-2** tells us that Antichrist cannot be revealed until the Restrainer is taken out of the way. The Restrainer is the Holy Spirit in His ministry through the church. Once the church is Raptured, Satan can produce his masterpiece—the Antichrist.

When ye therefore shall see

Many liberal scholars tell us that this prophecy was fulfilled in 170 BC by the Seleucid ruler Antiochus Epiphanes. In that year, he brought an army against Jerusalem and besieged it. Antiochus stopped the Jewish daily sacrifices in the Temple; offered a pig's blood on the Temple altar; sprayed swine's broth on the Temple walls; killed more than 100,000 Jews; and set up an image of Zeus in the Holy Place of the Temple for the Jews to worship. This historical account can be found in the first chapter of the apocryphal book of 1 Maccabees. It is from the cleansing of the Temple after its desecration by Antiochus that the Jews today still celebrate Hanukkah. The Lord Jesus Himself celebrated this Jewish patriotic remembrance. **John 10:22** However, the Lord Jesus is speaking in the future tense, some two hundred years AFTER Antiochus had already desecrated the Temple in Jerusalem. Antiochus was merely an historical type of the anti-Semite character that has been with the world since the Beginning of the Word of God. We have seen the Pharaohs of Egypt attempt to drown the Israelites out of existence. **Exodus 1:15-21** There was also the Persian purge of Haman in the Book of Esther. History tells us of the Spanish Inquisition, the Russian pogroms, the Nazi Holocaust, etc. THE Antichrist will be the most monstrous anti-Semite in world history. At the midpoint of the Tribulation Period, Antichrist will set up an image of himself in the Temple, and make all men to worship it and him. **2 Thessalonians 2:4; Revelation 13:5-15** This was prophesied in **Psalm 79:1.**

The Abomination of Desolation

The Lord Jesus moves from general signs of the first half of the Tribulation Period to a SPECIFIC sign that will begin the second half of the Tribulation Period. He makes reference to **Daniel 9:27; Daniel 11:31;** and **Daniel 12:11** where Daniel the prophet uses this same term. The sign of the **Abomination of Desolation** is when the Antichrist proclaims himself as a god, and places himself at the center of all Jewish worship in the rebuilt Temple. **2 Thessalonians 2:4** This is the sign that Jewish believers will recognize. This event ushers in the Great Tribulation.

(whoso readeth, let him understand)

This parenthetical insert shows that the Jewish believers of the Tribulation Period WILL recognize this sign. They will know what to do when these things come to pass. This abomination of desolation will start the Great Tribulation. Many conservative evangelicals have been stockpiling Hebrew-language New Testaments in the rock-hewn city of Petra, in modern-day Jordan, in anticipation of this event. This is where many conservative scholars believe the Jewish remnant will flee to in the last days. **Zechariah 14:5; Isaiah 63:1; Daniel 11:41; Revelation 12:14**

Daniel the Prophet

The Lord Jesus knew that His Jewish disciples had a working knowledge of Old Testament prophecy. He uses Daniel's fantastic prophecy of the Seventy Weeks from **Daniel 9:24-27**. The coming prince will sign a seven-year peace treaty with the nation of Israel. This will start the clock ticking again on this time element for the Jewish people. Halfway through that treaty, the Antichrist (coming prince) will break that covenant. He will make the Jews stop their reinstituted Temple worship. We know from Scriptures that this will be exactly halfway through this seven-year period. They give us the time element in **Daniel 7:25; Daniel 12:7; Revelation 11:2; Revelation 12:6; Revelation 12:14.** Scriptures tell us that this period is exactly three and a half years. It is called forty-two months; (**Revelation 11:2; Revelation 13:5**) 1260 days; (**Revela-**

tion 11:3; Revelation 12:6) and times, time and half a time. (**Daniel 12:7; Revelation 12:14**) This final three and a half years of the Tribulation Period will begin the GREAT Tribulation for the Jewish believers in the Coming Messiah. **2 Thessalonians 2** and **Revelation 13:12-18** refer to the beginning of the Great Tribulation Period and the reign of the Antichrist.

> Then let them which be in Judaea flee into the mountains.
>
> [Matthew 24:16]

Let them which be in Judaea

The use of several words by the Lord Jesus show that He is clearly NOT talking to the church in this message. He is speaking to the Jewish people, and especially to those Jewish believers of the last part of this age. He is speaking here specifically to those in Judaea.

Flee

The Lord Jesus emphasized the need for haste in those last days. Once the Beast has desecrated the temple, it will be foolish to fall behind for ANY reason. The flight of these Jewish believers is recorded in **Revelation 12:6-17**.

Into the mountains

The Lord Jesus is saying, "head for the hills."
Many conservative scholars see in this description the city of Petra. They quote the Biblical passages **Isaiah 16:1; Obadiah 1:3; Revelation 12:6**
to show the possibility of the Lord using Petra to
house His elect in the last days. This could all happen in conjunction with the Russian invasion of
Israel recorded in **Ezekiel 38-39**. The armies of a
Russian and Arabic/Muslim confederation are en-
camped on the mountains of Israel, awaiting the sig-
nal to move in for the kill. The Lord God in Heaven
sends fire down from Heaven to protect the apple of
His eye—Jerusalem. **Zechariah 2:8** The Russian-
led army is destroyed so that only one out of six soldiers leaves the battlefield alive. **Ezekiel 39:2** At this
time, Antichrist takes credit for this deliverance. We
know that he can call down fire from Heaven. **Revelation 13:13** This is when he will proclaim himself
god to the Israelites, set up his image in the Temple,
and force the Jews to worship him as god. **2 Thessalonians 2** The Lord Jesus tells His believers that
when all this happens, "head for the hills."

> Let him which is on the housetop not come down
> to take any thing out of his house.
>   [Matthew 24:17]

Let him which is on the housetop

Here is another reference to Hebrew culture. **Deuteronomy 22:8** gives instruction to the Jews to leave a border around their housetop. Why would God give a command like this? The housetops of the Jewish people were like the front porch of our day. They would sit on the housetop in the cool of a summer's evening to get relief from the heat of the day. The Lord Jesus says that if you hear of the abomination of desolation while they were relaxing, do not even go down into their house to get anything out. Run immediately. Isaiah the prophet made mention of this in **Isaiah 22:1.**

> **Neither let him which is in the field return back to take his clothes.**
> **[Matthew 24:18]**

Return back to take his clothes

The Lord Jesus repeats the immediacy of the situation. If a farmer is in the middle of a row and hears the news, he is not to go to the end of the row and get his coat he left there when it started to get hot that day. This is how serious that time will be for the Jewish people. The FINAL holocaust has begun!

> **And woe unto them that are with child, and to them that give suck in those days!**
> **[Matthew 24:19]**

With child

This shows the Lord Jesus' great concern and compassion for mothers and children. **Matthew 19:14** Women with small children will not be able to move very rapidly to flee as the time of the end draws near. Pregnancies will also slow down the movement of ladies and their husbands.

> But pray ye that your flight be not in the winter, neither on the sabbath day.
>
> [**Matthew 24:20**]

Pray that your flight not be in winter

Cold weather will hamper rapid movement in that day. Also, for Israel, the winter is the flood season. Small wadis one can step over in the spring become raging torrents that will become impossible to cross on foot in the winter time. And if there is snow on the ground in the day of the abomination, it will make following the fleeing Jews much easier, as they will leave tracks in the snow. This will allow the Beast's Secret Service henchmen to hunt them down like dogs.

Neither on the Sabbath day

Once again, the Sabbath is a sign that this discourse is for the Jewish people. The Sabbath was exclusively for the Jews. **Exodus 16:29** The Lord

Jesus is saying the religious scruples would hamper the Jews' flight if that day came on a Sabbath. The rabbis interpreted the Law to say that a Jewish person could only travel one mile on the Sabbath day. In the Book of Nehemiah, the Scriptures tell us that the city of Jerusalem was to be closed up on the Sabbath day. **Nehemiah 13:19** If that happens, the Jews will be trapped like rats. The Antichrist will have them where he wants them.

> **For then shall be great tribulation, such as was not since the beginning of the world to this time, no, nor ever shall be.**
>
> **[Matthew 24:21]**

For then shall be Great Tribulation

The Jews knew well of this time period. In the Old Testament, the most common name for this time was **the day of the LORD.** This title is used some twenty-four times in prophetic Scripture, and is referred to in other terms as well. It is variously called **that day; time of Jacob's trouble; the day of Jehovah; the day**; and other titles. The Old Testament prophets saw this as a time period in which God's wrath would be poured out in the Earth because of human sin. This same phrase is repeated in **Revelation 7:14** to refer to the same time period that the Lord Jesus was speaking of here. This period of the Great Tribulation is recorded in **Revelation 12-19**. The Jewish people have always been the object of hate, scorn, ridicule, and the object of persecution. THIS Tribulation will be different. It is far worse and far greater than any persecution the Jewish people have ever undergone before. The Lord Jesus Himself named this period. It is the final three and a half weeks of Daniel's Seventieth Week. Satan will be given full control of planet Earth. God will use the Antichrist to pour out His wrath. The Jewish people will be brought finally to the end of their rejection and disbelief in the Messiah. This period of Great Tribulation was prophesied as early as Moses in **Deuteronomy 4:30**. It is seen throughout the Word of God, and called several different names, such as **the last days; the Day of the Lord; the great day; that day**; etc. **Daniel 12:1; Mark 13:19**

No, nor ever shall be

Some liberals say that we are going through the Great Tribulation right now. This is contrary to the words of the Lord Jesus. He said that the Great Tribulation will be the worst time in history for His elect people the Jews. **Jeremiah 30:7** uses some of the same language the Lord Jesus uses to describe the severity of the persecution of the Great Tribulation.

**Alas! for that day is great, so that none is like it:
it is even the time of Jacob's trouble; but he shall
be saved out of it.**

Nothing in history will compare to the time of
tragedies that await mankind during the Great Tribulation. **Joel 2:2**

**And except those days should be shortened,
there should no flesh be saved: but for the elect's
sake those days shall be shortened.**
                                            [Matthew 24:22]

Except those days be shortened

This is a great statement from the Lord Jesus.
It shows us how much an unbelieving world owes
to the presence of believers in its midst. **Genesis
19:15-24** tells us the story of Lot among Sodom.
God's angels could do no harm to the wicked city
until Lot and his family were safely away from the
city of Sodom. The fact that of the presence of believers in the Gospel of the Coming King in the last
days assure that the world will NOT be completely
destroyed by the Antichrist.

There should no flesh be saved

From what we can glean from Scripture, less
than half of the people entering the Tribulation Period will survive those seven years. According to the

Lord Jesus, if He did not return to stop the blood-bath, there would not be one living person on Earth when He returned. The post tribulation position is not logical. Christian believers are looking for the Blessed Hope of **Titus 2:13.** Where would be the Blessed Hope in the Antichrist; the Battle of Armageddon; in the death of half of the world's population? The hope of the believer in this age is the return of Christ in the Rapture to take His people home BEFORE all this Tribulation is poured out on the Earth. **1 Thessalonians 1:10**

For the elect's sake those days shall be shortened

This refers to God's original elect people—the Jews. God promised that NO anti-Semite would ever be able to wipe the Jewish people from the face of the Earth entirely. God promised to leave a remnant of Israel for the population of His Millennial Kingdom. **Romans 11:5** The Lord Jesus will make sure His promise to Abraham is kept. **Genesis 12:1-3** The Lord will NEVER break a covenant He has made with ANY of His people.

> Then if any man shall say unto you, Lo, here *is* Christ, or there; believe *it* not.
>
> [**Matthew 24:23**]

Lo, Here is Christ

As the Lord Jesus had already warned, there will be false messiahs in the last days. **Matthew 24:5**

> **For there shall arise false Christs, and false prophets, and shall shew great signs and wonders; insomuch that, if** *it were* **possible, they shall deceive the very elect.**
>
> **[Matthew 24:24]**

For there shall arise false christs

There have always been people claiming to be the Jewish Messiah. They have been around since the beginning of the church age. **Acts 8:9-23** tells us the story of a Simon Magus who pretended to be a false miracle-working christ. The Romans brought destruction to Jerusalem in AD 70 because of the work of a false messiah named Bar Kochba. At that time, Rome had had enough of false messiahs, and destroyed the Jewish capital and its religion.

Shall show great signs and wonders

According to the Lord Jesus, the ability to work signs and wonders should be looked upon with suspicion. Faith healers and miracle-workers are NOT sure signs that the person is sent from God. We are to believe the Word of God rather than signs and wonders. The next great miracle-worker will NOT be Christ, according to the Lord Jesus. He will be

Antichrist. He will be able to work some great signs and wonders to deceive the masses of humanity. **Revelation 13:13-14; 2 Thessalonians 2:10-12; Matthew 24:11; Mark 13:22; 1 Timothy 4:1; 2 Timothy 4:3; 2 Peter 2:1**

The very elect

Millions of Jews will believe in the Gospel of the Kingdom that will be preached during the Tribulation Period. **Revelation 7** They will recognize the Old Testament signs, because they will know and believe the Torah and the Tanakh, (the Jewish Old Testament Scriptures).

> **Behold, I have told you before.**
>
> **[Matthew 24:25]**

I have told you before

The Lord Jesus did not want His people to be surprised. He wanted the Jewish people to understand and recognize the signs that would immediately precede His Coming.

> **Wherefore if they shall say unto you, Behold, he is in the desert; go not forth: behold, *he is* in the secret chambers; believe *it* not.**
>
> **[Matthew 24:26]**

He is in the desert

There will be rumors that the Messiah has already come. The world will be looking to the Antichrist as the true messiah. Even many of the elect will succumb to the performance of these false miracles the Antichrist will accomplish. Many of these signs and wonders will be done by the Antichrist's second-in-command, the False Prophet. He is the second beast of **Revelation 13.** The Dragon (Satan—Anti-Father), the Beast (the Antichrist—Anti-Son), and the False Prophet (Anti-Spirit) will make up the unholy, Satanic trinity of the last days. **Revelation 16:13**

Go not forth

People will travel hundreds and thousands of miles to see a false miracle, yet they will not travel down to the end of the block to hear the preached and proclaimed Word of God! Not long ago, a woman in a suburb of Atlanta claimed to have heavenly apparitions of the Virgin Mary on the same date of every month. Hundreds of people made the monthly pilgrimage to her house. It was a circus-like carnival atmosphere. Medallions and commemorations of all kinds were sold. The local news media showed up to hear what the Virgin Mary was saying every month. It finally died down and was not heard from again. The Lord Jesus warned against jumping on the bandwagon of every false prophet. He was telling true believers in all ages not to be deceived, and not to waste their time.

Believe it not

The Second Coming of Christ will be a visible event. There is a teaching going around in liberal circles that the Coming of the Lord happened in a secret event in the destruction of Jerusalem in AD 70. According to the Lord Jesus, even His enemies will be able to see Him. **Revelation 1:7** They cannot deny His appearing at last. There will be no secret Second Coming. The Lord Jesus told His followers that He will come with the clouds in judgment.

> **For as the lightning cometh out of the east, and shineth even unto the west; so shall also the coming of the Son of man be.**
>
> **[Matthew 24:27]**

As lightning cometh out of the east

A lightning storm is extremely public! There is nothing secret about lightning. It lights up the entire sky with a brief flash of blinding light. The Lord's Second Coming will be like that. The Heavens will be ablaze with a flash of the Glory of God. **Revelation 1:7; Zechariah 12:10** Unbelievers will miss the Rapture, but they cannot deny the Second

Coming. EVERYBODY on Earth will be an eye-witness to that event. The Second Coming of the Lord will also be with the speed of lightning. **Psalm 144:6; Zechariah 9:14; Luke 17:24** It will happen as quickly as lightning flashes across the darkened sky. There will be no time to repent at the day of judgment. All men will be caught red-handed in their sin and petty excuses for rejecting the Saviour when they meet Him Face-to-face.

> **For wheresoever the carcase is, there will the eagles be gathered together.**
>
> **[Matthew 24:28]**

Wheresoever the carcase is

The Lord's Return will mean the slaughter of millions of unbelievers at the Battle of Armageddon. **Revelation 19:21** The entire period of terror and horror will culminate in an epic battle of good versus evil—of God versus man. It is what the human poets have written about for centuries. And in the final battle, God wins.

There will the eagles be gathered together

In Palestine, they call eagles what we refer to as vultures. These are carrion birds that eat of the flesh of dead and decaying bodies. Millions of birds of prey are called to the Battle of Armageddon. This battle is referred to from God's viewpoint as **the supper of the great God. Revelation 19:17-18** The picture is of God Himself setting a table of a lost humanity for the birds of prey upon which they may gorge themselves. These carrion birds fly over the heads of an already doomed army, croaking and snapping at their heads. Job said about eagles in **Job 39:30**

> **Her young ones also suck up blood: and where the slain *are*, there *is* she.**

It is a perfect description of the Battle of Armageddon.

> **Immediately after the tribulation of those days shall the sun be darkened, and the moon shall not give her light, and the stars shall fall from heaven, and the powers of the heavens shall be shaken.**
>
> **[Matthew 24:29]**

Immediately after the tribulation

There is Good News for the believers in the Coming King. Christ's return will END the reign of Antichrist and the Great Tribulation, and BEGIN the reign of the Messiah and the Millennial Kingdom! The Old Testament is full of prophetic promises of the thousand-year reign of the Messiah. Satan's rule on planet Earth will come to an abrupt end at the appearing of the Messiah. His sway over men will end immediately!

Sun…moon…stars

The Word of God foretells of cataclysmic signs in the Heavens that would precede the appearing of the Messiah. They include **Isaiah 13:9-10; Isaiah 24:23; Ezekiel 32:7-8; Joel 2:31; Joel 3:15; Amos 5:20; Amos 8:9; Zephaniah 1:15; Mark 13:24; Luke 21:25; Revelation 6:12;** and **Revelation 8:12**, just to quote a few.

The powers of the heavens shall be shaken

The Word of God prophesies the shaking of the heavens. **Joel 3:16; Haggai 2:6; Revelation 12:9** This includes the heavenly bodies, such as stars, moon and the sun. However, it also has an application for the last days. This is a shaking of the power of Satan, who is called the prince of the power of the air. **Ephesians 2:2** This also refers to the power of Satan coming to an end in the heavenlies, and is cast into the Earth during the last days. **Revelation 12:12** Satan's domain is the heavenly places of the Earth, where his demons and minions tempt men today. Before the Second Coming of the Messiah, this power is destroyed. **Ephesians 6:12** The Resurrection of the Lord Jesus broke this power for all believers in His Resurrection. **Colossians 2:15**

And then shall appear the sign of the Son of man in heaven: and then shall all the tribes of the earth mourn, and they shall see the Son of man coming in the clouds of heaven with power and great glory.

[Matthew 24:30]

Then shall appear

This is described in its fullest detail in **Revelation 19:11-21.**

Sign of the son of man in heaven

The sign of the appearing of the Messiah to the Jewish people will be the Shekinah Glory of God! No other nation in history except the nation of Israel ever had the presence of the Shekinah as a manifestation of the visible presence of God among His people. It first appeared when Moses set up the Tabernacle according to the Word of God. **Exodus 40:34** It was a cloud that received the Lord Jesus into Heaven in the sight of His disciples on the top of the Mount of Olives. **Acts 1:9** A cloud of glory MUST accompany His return to Earth. **Matthew 26:64** The Shekinah was a sign of the appearing of the Messiah in Old Testament prophecy. **Daniel 7:13-14** It was also known to the Apostle Paul, and related to the believers in Rome as a sign of the Lord's return. **Romans 11:26** The high priest at the Lord Jesus' mock trial knew this prophecy, and tore his robes when the Lord Jesus claimed to be the Messiah. **Matthew 26:64-65** The disciples saw the Shekinah Glory of God in the Person of the Lord Jesus, and by this sign, they recognized Who the Lord Jesus was. **John 1:14; Matthew 17:2; 2 Peter 1:16** The sign of the Shekinah returning to the Earth was a sign for every believing Jew that the Day of the Lord's Wrath was over. The King is Coming!

The tribes of the Earth

This is a reference to the twelve Tribes of Israel. We refer to the Lost Tribes of Israel, but they are NOT lost. God knows where each and every tribe is. At least one representative of every one of the twelve tribes of Israel will be eyewitness to His Second Coming. **Zechariah 12:10**

Coming in the clouds of Heaven

This is the physical appearing of the Shekinah Glory of God back to Earth! It will be visible to every human eye. **Daniel 7:13; Matthew 26:61; Acts 1:9; Revelation 14:14**

> **And he shall send his angels with a great sound of a trumpet, and they shall gather together his elect from the four winds, from one end of heaven to the other.**
>
> **[Matthew 24:31]**

He shall send his angels

Angels are special ministers of the Second Coming of Christ. **2 Thessalonians 1:7-8; Matthew 13:41-49; Psalm 107:3; Matthew 25:31; Revelation 14:15** The angels will gather a BELIEVING remnant to Jehovah's Land to initiate a population in the Millennial Kingdom. **Ezekiel 37; Daniel 7:2; Revelation 7:1**

With a great sound of a trumpet

This is NOT the trumpet of the Rapture. What would a trumpet mean to a Jewish audience experiencing tribulation of the last days? The feast of the trumpet was one of Israel's commemorative feasts in the Old Testament. It is found in the list of annual feasts in **Leviticus 23:23-25**. Typically, this feast points to the prophecy of the Coming of the Messiah. All of Old Testament Israel was looking for the Messiah at the annual Feast of Trumpets. In the Old Testament, the trumpet is used in connection with the appearing of the Messiah. **Isaiah 11:11-12; Isaiah 27:13; Jeremiah 16:14-16** The prophetic aspect of the Feast of Trumpets is fulfilled as the Messiah appears. The Millennial Reign of the Messiah will begin. The trumpet was also used to call Israel into battle. **Numbers 10:10; Joshua 6:5** The Great Tribulation will be a battle for the Jewish remnant awaiting the Coming of the Messiah-King.

The trumpet was also used as a symbol for the Voice of God. **Exodus 19:19; Revelation 1:10** This will be the Voice of God proclaiming to the faithful Jewish that the Messiah-King has come at last!

They shall gather together

Moses told of a scattering of the nation of Israel because of sin. But he also told of a regathering of the nation of Israel to the Promised Land when the nation's faith would be made sight, and they will see the Messiah. The prophecy of this regathering is found in **Deuteronomy 30:3-5**, which says,

> That then the LORD thy God will turn thy captivity, and have compassion upon thee, and will return and gather thee from all the nations, whither the LORD thy God hath scattered thee. If *any* of thine be driven out unto the outmost *parts* of heaven, from thence will the LORD thy God gather thee, and from thence will he fetch thee: And the LORD thy God will bring thee into the land which thy fathers possessed, and thou shalt possess it; and he will do thee good, and multiply thee above thy fathers.

His elect

The rebirth of the nation of Israel in 1948 was heralded as a major significant fulfillment of Biblical prophecy. It was, but it was NOT a fulfillment of the prophecy of the regathering of Israel in the last days. There is one major difference. The 1948 regathering was in unbelief. Jewish people from all over the world are returning to their ancestral home in the nation of Israel. However, most of those returning are doing so in a state of unbelief in the Lord Jesus as Messiah. In fact, many Jews who are returning to Israel today are devout atheists, who do not even believe in the existence of God. The prophetic regathering the Lord Jesus spoke of is of a nation in belief of the Messiah, because they will believe all the signs of His Coming. They will have experienced that all in the last days of the Great Tribulation.

From the four winds

This was a familiar phrase and promise to the Jews. The Old Testament spoke of a regathering of the nation of Israel from the four corners of the Earth. **Ezekiel 37:9; Isaiah 43:5-6**

This part of the Olivet Discourse summarizes MANY Old Testament prophecies. **Daniel 9:24** tells us that one reason for Christ's Second Coming is **to seal up the vision and prophecy.** In other words, He will fulfill ALL unfulfilled prophecy to the nation of Israel. For the Jews, all prophecy culminates in the Messiah's Millennial Kingdom. God WILL keep His Word to His people. But the study of prophecy should also call the believer of today to a holy lifestyle. Let us be occupied in the Lord's work until He comes.

CHAPTER THREE

THE DAYS OF NOAH

MATTHEW 24:32-42

Now learn a parable of the fig tree; When his branch is yet tender, and putteth forth leaves, ye know that summer *is* nigh:
[Matthew 24:32]

The parable of the fig tree opens this section of the Lord's Olivet Discourse. This section has been misused by those who have attempted to set a date for the Rapture. Remember, the Rapture is NOT a subject of the Olivet Discourse. Date-setters say that the rebirth of Israel in 1948 was the blossoming of the fig tree. Some also believe that a generation is a forty-year period. According to this theory, the Rapture would surely take place in 1988. One the best-selling books of the late 1980s was a book by Edgar Wisenant that gave eighty-eight reasons why the Lord would come back in 1988. The Rapture did not take place in 1988. Undaunted, Wisenant wrote a sequel with eighty-nine reasons why the Lord would come again in 1989. With Wiesnant already proving to be a false prophet, the sequel STILL sold thousands of copies. This kind of anti-Biblical date-setting hurts the cause of Christ. It causes the lost to laugh and scoff at preachers and witnesses of the Gospel. We must learn to rightly divide the Word of Truth. **2 Timothy 2:15**

Learn a parable

A parable is an Earthly story with a Heavenly meaning. The Lord Jesus used the teaching style of parables in order that His listeners might understand what He was saying. The Lord Jesus is saying here that the fig tree that was cursed and died under the Creator's curse (**Matthew 21:18-20**) will one day come back to life.

Of the fig tree

The fig tree is a well-known Biblical symbol for the nation of Israel. We see it in passages such as **Hosea 9:10; Joel 1:7; Haggai 2:19; Jeremiah 24; Luke 13:6-9; Luke 21:29;** and **John 1:48**. The fig tree is also used as a symbol of destruction in the Day of the Lord, or the Tribulation Period. These passages include **Isaiah 34:4; Jeremiah 8:13; Joel 1:12; Habakkuk 3:17;** and **Revelation 6:13.** Actually, the Bible uses three different trees to symbolize the nation of Israel. John Phillips wrote that these three trees are used to represent different time periods on Israel's history. 1) The vine. This represents the nation of Israel from the call of Abraham to the rejection of the Messiah. **Isaiah 5:1-7; Matthew 21:33-44;** and **John 15:1-6** 2) The olive tree. This represents the nation after the return of the Messiah and in national repentance. **Romans 11** 3) The fig tree. This represents the nation of Israel from the rejection of its Messiah until it accepts Christ. The Lord Jesus' cursing of the fig tree in **Matthew 21** is both a miracle and a prophecy. Just after symbolic cursing of the fig tree, the Messiah cursed the nation that would soon reject Him. **Matthew 23:23-39**

Putteth forth leaves

The Lord Jesus said that Israel would produce leaves, but no fruit. Since 14 May, 1948, Israel has been alive and blooming again, but is producing no fruit. Israel today is still in unbelief and rejecting the Messiah. Theodore Hertzl, the founder of Zionism, was a secular humanist. He was a Jew by birth only, not by religious belief. But even in unbelief, life IS there, and God will once again deal with the nation of Israel, His chosen people. He will pick up with the nation of Israel where He left off at the insertion of the church age, and the completion of Daniel's Sixty-ninth Week.

So likewise ye, when ye shall see all these things, know that it is near, even at the doors.
$$\text{[Matthew 24:33]}$$

So likewise ye

The Lord Jesus gives us the application. Israel is NOW returning to the land in unbelief. It shows that the end of this age is near.

All these things

What things? The events of the Tribulation Period that the Lord Jesus has referred to during His sermon. These include the Seven Seals, the Abomination of Desolation, and the signs of the Coming of the Messiah.

It is near

This is the Greek singular masculine pronoun. It is usually translated "he" in the Scriptures. It could be the Lord Jesus is referring to HIS Second Coming and the set-up of the Millennial Kingdom.

At the doors

Nothing could be closer than "at the door." When someone is knocking at the door, all you have to do is open the door, and that person knocking is inside and present. It will happen THAT quickly.

> Verily I say unto you, This generation shall not pass, till all these things be fulfilled.
>
> [Matthew 24:34]

This generation

The liberals say that the generation here the Lord Jesus was referring to was the generation of Jews that the Lord was speaking to at the time. They say that the judgment came in the form of the Roman army in A.D. 70. But all these signs did not happen at that time. There was no Shekinah Glory of God that heralded the Coming of the Messiah. This verse gives hope. There was no hope for that generation of Jews. They had already rejected the Messiah in their hearts. The Lord Jesus pronounced judgment of that generation in **Matthew 21:43**. What does the Lord mean then by the term "generation?" The Greek word here is *genea*, which is literally "race." The context here shows that the Lord Jesus is using "generation" to refer to the Jewish people, the Everlasting Nation of Israel. Despite a history of anti-Semitism, hatred, and ethnic cleansing, God has promised to preserve a remnant of His chosen people to enter into the Millennial Kingdom. Despite Pharaoh drowning Jewish male children in the Nile River; Haman issuing a proclamation to destroy all Jews in the Persian empire; Herod the Great attempting to murder all Jewish boys born

in Bethlehem; the Spanish Inquisition of Torque-
mada; and the holocaust of Adolph Hitler in the
1940s, God has PROMISED the nation of Israel it
WOULD survive until it sees the Messiah coming
in the Shekinah Glory of God. The Nazi holocaust
killed more than six million Jews, which was equiv-
alent to one-third of the population of Jews in the
entire world. Antichrist will attempt to complete
Hitler's Final Solution, and he will ALMOST succeed. Where Hitler killed one-third of the Jewish
population of the world, Antichrist will kill TWO-
thirds of the world's Jewish population. This actually gives hope to the Jewish remnant in the last days.
The Lord Jesus promises that the Jewish race WILL
make it through the Great Tribulation to see the
Promise of the Coming of the Messiah. This means
that God will keep His promises He made way back
to Abraham about his seed, the Jewish nation.

Shall not pass
This is a translation of the Greek words *ou me.*
This is the strongest possible term in the Greek lan-
guage for a negation. The Lord Jesus is saying, "by
NO means." It is a promise form the Lips of the
Lord Jesus that a remnant will witness His Return,
and the Old Testament promises of the Millennial
Kingdom will be fulfilled.

Heaven and earth shall pass away, but my words shall not pass away.

[Matthew 24:35]

Heaven and Earth shall pass away

New Testament believers already know this. Peter describes this in **2 Peter 3:10-13**. The Earth will be destroyed by fire, because the Lord promised Noah that it will never again be destroyed by a flood. **Genesis 9:11** The final Book in the Bible also tells us of a new Heaven and a new Earth, as does the prophet Isaiah. **Revelation 21:1; Isaiah 65:17; Isaiah 66:22.** I do not believe this planet will never be completely destroyed. I think it is too important to God to destroy it. This is the place where His Son shed His Blood on the Cross, and made atonement for the mystery of iniquity for human sin. But the Word of God tells us that the Earth and the Heavens WILL be purged by fire. This is because Satan brought sin into the universe, and Adam and Eve brought sin into the world. The universe must be purged of all sin before the Eternal State begins, because God will not exist in the presence of sin.

My Words shall not pass away

This is also promised elsewhere is Scripture. **Psalm 12:6; Isaiah 14:24; Isaiah 40:8; Daniel 9:24; Matthew 5:18; Mark 13:31; Luke 21:33;**

Hebrews 12:27; 1 Peter 1:23-25; 1 John 2:17
Here we are some two thousand years later, reading the SAME Words of the Lord Jesus. God's Word has been persecuted; hated; denied; mocked; attacked; belittled; and disbelieved by common man, scholar and noble. Yet here It stands! This shows not only the doctrine of Inspiration of the Scriptures, it also shows the doctrine of Preservation of the Scriptures. God Himself promised to preserve His Word. It also shows that the VERY Words of Scripture are inspired and preserved by God, not just the thoughts. God's Word is as inerrant and eternal as the Son of God Himself. One illustration from history will suffice. In the days of the French enlightenment lived a philosopher named Voltaire. He boasted that the new ideas of humanity would prevail, and that the words of Voltaire would eclipse the Word of God. Voltaire died an atheist. His death was attended by his nurse, who said that not for all the money in Europe would she attend the death of another infidel. He died screaming out for pain, expressing that flames were licking his body. He was tormented, and cursed God and man. He pleaded for help from the pain, but none came before he breathed his last. His home was turned into a museum. Nobody came to the museum, so it was sold. The French Bible Society bought his house, and turned it into a printing press for the publication

and distribution of French-language Bibles to all of
Europe. God's Word WILL survive.

> **But of that day and hour knoweth no *man*, no,
> not the angels of heaven, but my Father only.**
> **[Matthew 24:36]**

That day

This is a Scriptural term for the Day of the Lord,
or the Tribulation Period. This period encompasses
the time from the signing of the seven-year peace
treaty to the Second Coming of Christ. The exact
phrase "that day" is used throughout the Old Testament to refer to the Tribulation Period. I would
have liked to list all the Scripture passages that use
this term, but in a search, I found it used more than
fifty times in the Book of Isaiah alone! One of the
most well-known verses is **Jeremiah 30:7,** which
says,

> **Alas! for that day *is* great, so that none *is* like it: it
> *is* even the time of Jacob's trouble; but he shall be
> saved out of it.**

As we have seen, this is a reference to the Jews
going through the Great Tribulation. Notice that
the phrase **that day** is used by the prophets to describe that time period. **Isaiah 2:11-20** is one of
hundreds of Old Testament passages that used this

term to describe the final days of human history.

Day and hour

The date of all this is unknown on Earth or in Heaven, except by God the Father. In a parallel passage, the Lord Jesus said that even HE did not know the timing of the beginning of the Tribulation Period, or that day. **Mark 13:32** We need not to be convinced by modern-day "prophets" and date-setters who claim to know when the Tribulation Period will begin. Today's "prophets," according to the Words of the Lord Jesus Himself, know more than the Son of God Himself!

But My Father only

God the Father ONLY knows when the Day of the Lord will begin. HE has all authority over the End-Time events. The disciples asked the Lord Jesus if He would return the Kingdom to Israel before He went back to Heaven.

> **And he said unto them, It is not for you to know the times or the seasons, which the Father hath put in his own power.**
>
> **[Acts 1:7]**

We know WHAT will begin the Day of the Lord—the signing of the seven-year peace treaty

THE DAYS OF NOAH 67

between Antichrist and Israel—but we do not know WHEN it will happen. This verse should also give comfort and hope to the Jews of the last days. The Lord Jesus said in the verse above that the Father has the power over the end times. It may LOOK like Satan has control. It may SEEM as though Antichrist will succeed in elimination the Jewish race. But the One Who is in ultimate control is God the Father, and He has sent His Son to promise His people that a remnant WILL make it through the Day of the Lord to see the Messiah come in the Shekinah Glory of God.

> **But as the days of Noe *were*, so shall also the coming of the Son of man be.**
> **[Matthew 24:37]**

As the days of Noe were

The illustration of Noah fits right in with the Day of the Lord. **Luke 17:26; 1 Peter 3:20** What did the Lord Jesus mean? Noah lived at the close of one age. He preached judgment for one hundred and twenty years. He was saved, along with his house, through the judgment of the flood. He entered the beginning of a new age, and a New Earth. This is EXACTLY what will happen to Israel in the last days. The Jews will be living at the end of the Age of Grace. The Gospel of the Grace of the Lord Jesus

Christ has been preached for two thousand years. The Jews will be kept through the judgment of the Tribulation Period. Notice also that the Lord Jesus believed in the historicity and authenticity of the Book of Genesis, especially the first eleven chapters that the liberals are so quick to deny today.

So shall also

Christ's comparison to the days of Noah toll the death-knell to those who claim the Gospel will convert the world. Many liberals believe that after the conversion of the world to Christianity, then the Messiah will come. There are only two problems with this theory. History shows that the world has NOT become more Christianized. In fact, the world today is not becoming Christianized, it is becoming Islamized. More people are converting to the Islamic faith today than Christianity. The other reason why this theory cannot be true is that there is NO Scriptural basis for this theory. The Words of the Son of God here seem to imply the exact opposite of the liberal theory. The world, in the last days, will become farther and farther away from the Faith of Christianity toward selfishness. **Luke 18:8**

The Coming of the Son of Man be

The Second Coming of the Messiah is referred to one thousand eight-hundred forty-five times in the Word of God. It is mentioned in twenty-three of the twenty-seven New Testament Books, and is the last prophecy in the entire Word of God. **Revelation 22:20** The Second Coming is an extremely important doctrine to God, and is essential to the faith of millions of Christians and Jews.

> **For as in the days that were before the flood they were eating and drinking, marrying and giving in marriage, until the day that Noe entered into the ark,**
>
> **[Matthew 24:38]**

Eating and drinking

Day-after-day Noah labored on the ark. Every time his hammer hit a peg on the ark, it would proclaim to the antediluvian world, "judgment is coming." Night-after-night Noah would hold open-air crusades. Perhaps many people came at first to see the crazy old coot who proclaimed that judgment was coming. After all, he was preaching about a flood when it had never rained on the Earth. But after a while, the crowds dwindled. In the end, he was ignored. People were too busy to worry about crazy ol' Noah, and his wild preaching. People lived their lives as there were no such man as Noah, no such thing as coming judgment, or no such Person as God.

Marrying and giving in marriage

This human activity of the pursuit of pleasure will continue in the capitals of the world right until the time when God Himself destroys the humanistic governments of man. **Revelation 18:23**

> **And knew not until the flood came, and took them all away; so shall also the coming of the Son of man be.**
>
> [**Matthew 24:39**]

Knew not until the flood came

Why didn't the people of Noah's day know? **2 Peter 2:5** says that Noah was a preacher of righteousness. He preached for one hundred and twenty years with no conversions except his own family. God promised never to leave Himself without a witness on Earth. The people of Noah's day refused to listen to the Word of God. Because of their refusal to heed the Word of God, the Earth was destroyed. **Genesis 7:21**

So shall also the coming of the Son of man be

These words show that the same spirit of indifference and selfishness will permeate the society of the last days. There will be no care for faithful preaching nor fulfilled prophecy. Judgment was looming in the days of Noah, and an even greater judgment is looming in our own day!

> **Then shall two be in the field; the one shall be taken, and the other left.**
> **[Matthew 24:40]**

The one shall be taken

This is NOT the Rapture. Preachers and Bible teachers have used this verse for centuries to point to the Rapture. But we must look at the context of this verse to find the true meaning. The Greek word for taken here is *airo*. It is the same word that is used in **John 19:16,**

> **Then delivered he him therefore unto them to be crucified. And they took Jesus, and led *him* away.**

Where were they "taking" the Lord Jesus? The Romans were taking Him to the destruction and death of the Cross. Note also the words of the Lord Jesus in **verse 39** of this Chapter. "The flood came and TOOK them all away." Where did the Flood sweep these people who refused to listen to the preaching of Noah? Were they taken up to the clouds to meet the Lord in the air like Christian believers will be at the Rapture? Not hardly. They were killed by the judgment of the Flood, and were drowned. In Noah's day, nobody went to meet the

Lord Jesus in the air. Those who refused to believe the preaching of Noah were taken to destruction in the Flood, and those who believed Noah's preaching were taken safely through the judgment of the Flood in safety in the ark. But if you still doubt, let us look at a parallel passage in **Luke 17:34-37.**

> **I tell you, in that night there shall be *two* men in one bed; the one shall be taken, and the other shall be left. Two *women* shall be grinding together; the one shall be taken, and the other left. Two *men* shall be in the field; the one shall be taken, and the other left. And they answered and said unto him, Where, Lord? And he said unto them, Wheresoever the body *is*, thither will the eagles be gathered together.**

In this passage from the Gospel of Luke, in verse 37 the Lord Jesus answers the question as to where those taken in judgment will be taken. To a place where the eagles are gathered together to eat the rotting and decaying flesh of those who have been killed. The Lord Jesus here is definitely NOT talking about eternal bliss. He is speaking about being taken to judgment. What He is saying is that some will be taken in the judgment of the Great Tribulation, and some will enter the Glorious Millennial Reign of the Messiah. Some will be taken in death, and some will be left to enter the Millennium.

> Two *women shall be* grinding at the mill; the one
> shall be taken, and the other left.
>
> [Matthew 24:41]

Two women shall be grinding at the mill

This shows the universal nature of the judgment of God upon a God-rejecting world. It will encompass every aspect of society. In the previous verse, those in the field would face the judgment. This shows the work of men. This verse shows two women working. The judgment of God will fall of ALL those who reject His Word on the end times. It will fall on men and women; rich and poor; black and white; religious and pagan. All those who refuse the Gospel of the Coming King will face the judgment of God, just as all those who reject the Gospel of the Lord Jesus Christ face the judgment of God at the Great White Throne. **Revelation 20:11-15**

> Watch therefore: for ye know not what hour your
> Lord doth come.
>
> [Matthew 24:42]

Watch therefore

With a solemn warning, the Lord Jesus closes His predictions about the end of the Jewish Age. **Watch** means "to be ready." "To be ready," means "to be saved." It is a warning to His elect of the close of the age to make sure that they are believers before it is too late. The Word of God warns those in the last days to be ready for the Coming of the Messiah-King. **Matthew 26:41; Mark 13:37** In the Olivet Discourse, the Lord Jesus is talking about His Second Coming, and not the Rapture. He gives the Jews at the end of the age signs to look for that will herald His Appearing. The Rapture is a sign-less event. It could happen at any moment, or at any day. It is the Blessed Hope **(Titus 2:13)** of the Church today. We should live in constant expectation of the imminent trumpet sound of the Lord Jesus Coming for His Church. Are YOU ready? Where would YOU be if Christ came tonight?

CHAPTER FOUR

THE PARABLE OF THE UNFAITHFUL SERVANT

MATTHEW 24:43-51

The contents of this next section of our Lord's Olivet Discourse are entirely different from the preceding section. We have seen all our Lord's predictions related to Old Testament prophecy, as well as the Book of Revelation. Now, the Lord Jesus begins to speak in parables. This section consists of three distinct parables, and shows that between the Lord's Ascension and His Second Coming, there will be the true and the false; the saved and the unsaved. In His parable of the wheat and tares, (**Matthew 13:24-32**) the Lord will allow the tares to grow among the wheat until they are separated at the end of the age. Remember, the disciples asked what would be the characteristics of the world as the end of the age approached in **Matthew 24:3**. These three parables give the moral aspect of PROFESSING believers. Each parable is linked with the Lord's Coming, when HE Himself will distinguish between the good and the bad; between the true and the false; between the possessor and the professor.

> **But know this, that if the goodman of the house had known in what watch the thief would come, he would have watched, and would not have suffered his house to be broken up.**
> **[Matthew 24:43]**

In what watch the thief would come

The use of the word **thief** would mean something to the disciples, and people familiar with Bible prophecy would readily understand. It is a common imagery in Scripture used for the Lord's Second Coming. **Luke 12:39; 1 Thessalonians 5:2; 2 Peter 3:10; Revelation 3:3; Revelation 16:15** The term is always used in connection with judgment. It denotes a sudden, swift, unexpected and final judgment. This imagery makes the Second Coming of the Lord Jesus a fearful prospect for those who are unbelievers.

He would have watched

The Lord Jesus has just spent more than forty verses giving His disciples all the signs of His Second Coming. He also gave a very definite timetable of the Tribulation. He referred them back to the prophecy of the Seventy Weeks of **Daniel 9:24-27.** That time would have a very definite starting point—the signing of the seven-year peace treaty between the Antichrist and the nation of Israel. It also had a very definite mid-way point that the Lord spoke of in **verse 15**—the Abomination of Desolation, when the Antichrist sets up an image of himself in the Jewish Temple in Jerusalem, and causes all to worship him. From that time, those waiting on the Messiah would be able to count forty-two months, or even one thousand two hundred sixty days, until the appearing of the Messiah. **Revelation 12:6; Revelation 13:5** So if this Tribulation Period has a definite starting point and a definite ending time of exactly seven years, why will they not be able to figure out when the Coming of the Lord will be? The answer is as simple as it is tragic. Most people of that day will be taken by surprise by the Lord's appearing simply because they have chosen NOT to believe the Word of God! Remember, the Lord Jesus has warned His disciples that Satan's men would show so many signs and wonders that if it were possible, even the very elect of Israel would be deceived. **Matthew 24:24** But the Lord had given a warning—even if His people missed the signs—in **Luke 19:13.** He told them to **Occupy till I come**. It is as if He is saying, 'even if you miss the signs and mathematical computations, be about MY business until you see Me come in Glory.' If we are keeping busy in His service, His Coming will NOT take us by surprise.

**Therefore be ye also ready: for in such an hour as
ye think not the Son of man cometh.**
                              [**Matthew 24:44**]

Be ye also ready

How can the Jews of that day be ready for His
appearing? The first and primary way is to believe
the Word of God. The Word of God still has as Its
end the salvation of human souls. **2 Peter 3:9** The
BEST way to prepare to meet the Lord Jesus is to
take Him at His Word, believe what He said about
salvation, and accept His free offer of pardon for sin
through His Blood on the Cross of Calvary. That
will get you ready to meet the Lord Jesus, whether
in life, death, Rapture, or Second Coming.

The Son of Man

This is a title the Lord Jesus used of Himself fre-
quently in the Gospels. This title shows the Lord's
relationship to the Earth. It shows what the Lord
Jesus came to Earth to do. He came to Earth to re-
claim the dominion Adam forfeited in his fall. When
the LORD God created man, He gave him dominion over planet Earth, and ordered him to subdue the
planet. **Genesis 1:26-28** When Adam fell, he forfeited this dominion to Satan, who is now the god of
this world. **2 Corinthians 4:4** This title is used of the
Lord Jesus as early as **Daniel 7:13**, where the proph-

et sees a vision of the Son of Man approaching the
Ancient of Days and receiving the dominion to rule
and reign over planet Earth. As used in context here,
we must remember the Lord has been answering the
disciples questions about the End Times. He has told
them about the reign of Antichrist. In **verse 44**, He
used the title **Son of Man** to remind the disciples
that while the reign of Antichrist is raging on Earth,
it will not be permanent. He reminds the disciples of
all the glorious promises in the Old Testament about
the Millennial Kingdom, and the Reign of Messiah
on Earth. When Messiah returns, He WILL take the
kingdoms of this Earth away from Satan's man, and
rule with all the benevolence of Heaven on Earth.
He IS Coming Again to rule over ALL nations. Then,
and ONLY then, this world will experience the government that God intended for the Planet to have all
along, since the Garden of Eden. The Lord Jesus will
succeed where Adam failed.

> **Who then is a faithful and wise servant, whom
> his lord hath made ruler over his household, to
> give them meat in due season?**
> **[Matthew 24:45]**

Who then is a faithful

This means the servant is busy. He is devoted.
He is trusted. He is loyal. But most of all, he is obe-

dient. The Word of God tells us that "love" is a four-letter word, and it is spelled O-B-E-Y. **John 14:15** If we LOVE the Lord, we will OBEY the Lord. This servant loves his Master, and he willingly fulfills the task the Lord has requested of him. Because of this faithfulness, the Lord has guaranteed him a reward. **2 Corinthians 5:10** God is not looking for success in a dollar amount. He is looking for faithfulness.

Wise servant

This is a steward, or a butler. It is one who has been entrusted with all the goods of a master's home. This servant has earned his master's trust and confidence. Eliezer, the servant of Abraham, was entrusted with this office to find a wife for his master's son Isaac. **Genesis 24** What is the qualification for this important office? The answer is found in **1 Corinthians 4:2. Moreover it is required in stewards, that a man be found faithful.**

His lord hath made him ruler

The imagery the Lord Jesus uses here is quite obvious. The **lord** is the Coming Messiah, the **faithful servant** is the believing Jew, and the **evil servant** is the unbelieving Jew, who will be caught by surprise at the Appearing of the Messiah. Stewards of all ages are called to be faithful for their service to the Lord. **1 Corinthians 4:2**

Over his household

This shows the Jewish flavor of this parable, as well as the entire Olivet Discourse. The House is a well-known symbol for the nation of Israel. **Ezekiel 2:5; Matthew 10:6; Matthew 15:24** In **Matthew 23:38,** the Lord Jesus had just pronounced judgment on the nation of Israel by saying, **Behold, your house is left unto you desolate.** In **Matthew 13,** the Lord Jesus tells the famous mystery parables. It shows what the Kingdom of Heaven, the Rule of God on Earth, will be like. In the first verse of that chapter, we are told that the Lord Jesus went out of the house, and sat by the sea. The house is a symbol for the nation of Israel. The Lord Jesus knew that Israel would reject the Messiah, so He left the House. The sea is a symbol for the Gentile nations. **Revelation 17:15** The Lord Jesus from this point on offers the Gospel to the Gentile nations, since the Jews were given the FIRST opportunity to accept Messiah, but rejected Him. **Romans 1:16**

To give them meat in due season

The responsibility of ALL believers—regardless of the dispensation—is to feed others with the Word of God. God will make sure His people are fed. **Psalm 104:27; Psalm 145:15; Luke 12:42** The Word of God is fit for ANY child of God, whatever spiritual state in which he may be. The Word gives milk for the beginner, bread for the more advanced, and strong meat for the most mature. **1 Corinthians 3:2** It is through a knowledge of the Word of God that all spiritual maturity and growth flows. If you want to grow in the knowledge and grace of the Saviour, get in to the Word of God! **2 Peter 3:18**

> **Blessed *is* that servant, whom his lord when he cometh shall find so doing.**
>
> **[Matthew 24:46]**

Blessed is that servant

Why are we working? The faithful servant was working because he loved his Master. He is not working to be popular. He is not working to be successful in the eyes of the world. He is working to be obedient to his Master. The ONLY One he cares to please is his Master. He is concerned about being faithful in the Eyes of his Master.

Whom his lord when he cometh shall find so doing

Why is this servant faithful? Why is he working diligently? He is working in anticipation of his Lord's Coming. He has NOT forgotten the promise of his Master to Return one day. When we lose sight of our Blessed Hope (**Titus 2:13**), we become lazy and quit working for the Master. We should NEVER forget that the Lord promised to come for us one day.

> **Verily I say unto you, That he shall make him ruler over all his goods.**
>
> [**Matthew 24:47**]

He shall make him ruler

The faithful servant is promised a great reward. He is promised to rule and reign with his Master for one thousand years during the Millennial Kingdom. **Revelation 20:4** For an Israelite, this is THE highest possible reward. In the New Testament, all the promises to the church are tied into Heaven. But for the Jew, all the promises to the nation of Israel in the Old Testament are tied to the land of Israel, and especially during the time of the Millennial Reign of the Messiah. That is why Abraham bought a parcel of land in the Promised Land in which he buried his family. **Genesis 23:4** This is why Joseph, the second-most powerful man in the world at the time, requested his body to be taken and buried in the Promised Land, rather than to be buried in a magnificent pyramid. **Genesis 47:30** The patriarchs wanted to be buried in the Land of Israel so that when the bodily resurrection occurred, they would be there to see the Messiah in His Millennial Reign. The oldest book in the Word of God teaches the reality of a bodily resurrection, (**Job 19:25-27**) and it was the hope of ALL Israelites to live and reign with Messiah in His Millennial, Earthly Kingdom.

All his goods

The Lord Jesus will possess ALL the kingdoms on Earth at His Return. **Revelation 19:12** shows that He will be given the crowns of ALL dominion on Earth at His Appearing. Even now, God the Father has invested Him will ALL power (authority) on Heaven and Earth. **Matthew 28:18** Faithfulness in one area leads to increased responsibility in another area. Our Lord does not reward on the basis of amount of return. He does not reward on the basis of greatness in the eyes of the world. He rewards for faithfulness to Him.

> But and if that evil servant shall say in his heart, My lord delayeth his coming;
>
> [Matthew 24:48]

If that evil servant

This man was a part of the same household as the first servant. He was a Jew. He was given the same responsibility—to give out the Word of God. **Romans 3:2** Yet he had no right to this prestigious office. He had no faith in his Lord. Because he did not believe his Lord, the Lord's Return will take him by surprise. This servant will take the mark of the Beast. He will play the politician rather than the faithful servant. He will look to better his situation in this life while on Earth. He will choose the authority of Satan, and he will end up at the Great White Throne and land in the Lake of Fire for all eternity. He never really cared for the Messiah at all. All he cared about was himself.

Shall say in his heart

This is the key verse of the entire parable. It shows where the root of the problem is. The heart is where the real attitude is exposed. **Matthew 15:7-20** The evil servant's problem all began in his heart. He gave no heed to the Words of his Messiah. He did not store up God's Word in his heart. **Psalm 119:11** He became a scoffer. He may not have been an evil servant once, but he questioned his Lord's Words. When he did, Satan crept in. Satan will always creep in because Satan is a creep. Satan's first recorded words in the Scriptures are **Yea, hath God said ... ? Genesis 3:1** Satan has ALWAYS tried to get man to question and then deny the Word of God. Once the seed of doubt in God's Word is sown, it yields bitter fruit. Once this servant disbelieved God's Word, he gave himself to evil. If you reject the Truth, the only thing left to believe is a lie.

Delayeth his coming

The disciples expected the Lord to return in the first century of the church. Even the beloved apostle Paul expected to be taken in the Rapture. **1 Thessalonians 4:15** After some two thousand years now, many have given up the hope of His Return. Many Jews today are Jewish in birth, language and culture only. As a whole, they continue in a state of unbelief in the Messiah. Peter himself faced this problem in the first-century church. **2 Peter 3:3-4** Since the time of Peter, there have been those who have scoffed and laughed at the prospect of the Return of Christ to Earth. For the church, this has been going on for two thousand years. But for the Jew, many have been scoffing at the Promise of the Messiah's coming for nearly six thousand years now!

> **And shall begin to smite *his* fellowservants, and to eat and drink with the drunken;**
> **[Matthew 24:49]**

Shall begin to smite his fellowservants

The evil servant neglects his appointed ministry. He mistreats others. He becomes self-important; self-absorbed; and self-indulgent. He has set himself up as the ultimate authority in the place of God's Word. We do this ANY time we deny ANY part of the Word of God.

> **The lord of that servant shall come in a day when he looketh not for *him*, and in an hour that he is not aware of,**
> **[Matthew 24:50]**

In an hour that he is not aware of

Evil servants are not expecting the Messiah because they have rejected His Word. It has been so since the First Coming of the Messiah. **John 5:37-40** The ONLY way you can be ready for His Appearing is to take God at His Word. How do you get ready? Get SAVED! Then you will be assured of Heaven.

> **And shall cut him asunder, and appoint *him* his portion with the hypocrites: there shall be weeping and gnashing of teeth.**
> **[Matthew 24:51]**

Appoint

At Christ's Return, EVERYBODY will give an account of himself before the Lord Jesus. Believers will give an account of their stewardship since their salvation. Their salvation will NOT be in doubt at the Judgment Seat of Christ. **Romans 14:10; 2 Corinthians 5:10** That has already been taken care of at the judgment of the Cross. Unbelievers will also have to give an account of themselves. They will have to stand before the Great White Throne **(Rev-**

elation 20:11-15) and be judged for not accepting Christ as their Saviour. All men of all ages will be exposed, and be judged by the Lord Jesus Christ. **John 5:22** All the petty little excuses man hides behind today will be gone. "If there is a loving God, he won't send anybody to hell." "It doesn't matter what you believe, as long as you're sincere." "I believe in a God of love, not judgment." "There are many ways to God." "I'm just as religious as the next guy." "I'm doing the best I can." "God is not a narrow-minded god." All these excuses that seem so self-righteous to man today will pale away in the Light of the Face of the Lord Jesus Christ. Every mouth will be stopped, and they will realize that the Word of God was true after all. **Romans 3:19** But for the unbeliever, it will be everlastingly too late.

His portion

This servant had a wicked heart. He will spend eternity with his own kind. Many souls will be in hell that were once considered servants of God on Earth. There will be pastors in hell. There will be deacons in hell. There will be Sunday school teachers in hell. There will be singers in hell. Their HEARTS will betray them at last. They may have looked good to men every Sunday, but the Lord Jesus judges the heart. **1 Samuel 16:7** There will be no fooling God on that day, for He does not look at what you do.

He looks at WHY you do it. Do you do things for the praise of man, or do you do things for the Eyes of your Master alone. Scripture teaches us that God sees what is in the Heart.

Hypocrites

This is the Greek word for "actor." It is somebody who pretends to be something he is not. Many people CLAIM to be believers. No doubt on Judgment Day, the evil servant will point to all the shady business deals that came out in his Master's favor. We find the Lord's sobering, heart-breaking answer in **Matthew 7:21-23**,

> **Not every one that saith unto me, Lord, Lord, shall enter into the kingdom of heaven; but he that doeth the will of my Father which is in heaven. Many will say to me in that day, Lord, Lord, have we not prophesied in thy name? and in thy name have cast out devils? and in thy name done many wonderful works? And then will I profess unto them, I never knew you: depart from me, ye that work iniquity.**

There shall be weeping

This carries the idea of grief. In hell, they will remember all the squandered opportunities to accept Christ as their Saviour. They will realize that their judgment is just. For all eternity, they will have the sad realization that their day of salvation is past, never to be given the opportunity again. This same description of hell is also given in **Matthew 13:42** and **Matthew 25:30.**

Gnashing of teeth

This carries the idea of everlasting torment and unending pain. The Lord Jesus KNEW the reality of hell. He tried to warn men of the reality, severity and eternality of hell. He preached twice as much about hell as He did about Heaven. That tells us how important the subject of hell was to Him. The term **gnashing of teeth** is used throughout the Word of God to signify the reality of a place of eternal torment away from the presence of God. **Psalm 112:10; Matthew 8:12; Matthew 22:13; Luke 13:28**

According to the Lord Jesus, your belief in the Second Coming is directly linked to your belief in His First Coming. If you believe in the reality and work of the Lord's First Coming, you will believe in the reality and work of the Lord's Second Coming. We should beware of ANY teaching that has the faintest hint of delaying OR denying the Lord's Second Coming. The author of all such doctrine is Satan. Also notice that the Lord Jesus only gave two possibilities for reward—reward for faithful service and sorrow for evil service. Likewise, there are only two options for eternity—Heaven or hell. Where will YOU be for all eternity?

CHAPTER FIVE

THE PARABLE OF THE TEN VIRGINS

MATTHEW 25:1-13

The parable of the wise and foolish virgins is well-known, and perhaps much-abused. The context shows that the timing of this parable is in the post-rapture period. It must be understood in that context. After the Rapture, God will revert to His Old Testament way of dealing with people through the coming and going of the Holy Spirit. He will go back to using the nation of Israel to be a witness to the Gentile nations. The church age is a clearly-marked parenthesis inserted between Daniel's Sixty-Ninth and Seventieth Week. It is a parenthesis that began on the Day of Pentecost, and will end at the Rapture.

> **Then shall the kingdom of heaven be likened unto ten virgins, which took their lamps, and went forth to meet the bridegroom.**
>
> **[Matthew 25:1]**

The Kingdom of Heaven

What would the Jewish believers of the end times understand this phrase to mean? The Kingdom of Heaven is a term used exclusively in the New Testament in the Gospel of Matthew. The Gospel of Matthew was a Gospel written from the Hebrew perspective. It proclaims that the long-awaited Messiah has finally come. It presents the Lord Jesus Christ as the Son of David. **Matthew 1:1** The Kingdom of Heaven is used specifically of the time of the Millennial Reign of the Messiah. It is the time when the King of Heaven will literally set up His Throne on the Earth, and reign in perfect righteousness and justice on planet Earth. It is the time that was the culmination of all Old Testament prophecy for the nation of Israel. It was the high-water mark of the history of the nation of Israel. The prophets saw this time as when the wolf would lay down with the lamb. **Isaiah 11:6.** The coming Kingdom of Heaven on Earth included the resurrection of the body. **Job 19:25-26** This is why all the patriarchs all wanted to be buried in the Promised Land, because they wanted to enjoy the Millennial Kingdom—the Kingdom of the Reign of God Himself—in their Resurrected Bodies. **Genesis 25:9; Genesis 49:29-30; Genesis 50:24-25** This is what the nation of Israel would understand by the term the Kingdom of Heaven.

Ten

The Lord Jesus appears, as do ten virgins. Ten is a number that is often associated with the nation of Israel. God gave the nation of Israel the Ten Commandments on the top of Mount Sinai. **Exodus 20:1-17** It took ten male members to institute a synagogue in the time of Paul. When Boaz wanted to purchase the field of his near kinsman, and also his widow Ruth, it took ten men to witness a legal contract. **Ruth 4:2**

Virgins

These virgins are NOT the church. They are part of the wedding party. They would be what we call "bridesmaids" today. They are not a part of the Bride. The church is the Bride. **Ephesians 5:25-28** These virgins are not in the Rapture. Many will be saved after the Rapture of the church. **Revelation 7** They will not be in the church. They will miss the Rapture, but they WILL be in the Millennial Kingdom. During the Tribulation Period, they will be looking diligently for the Coming King. At least the WISE ones will be looking for the Coming King. It is thought that John Baptist MAY be the best man in this wedding party because of the Lord Jesus' words in **John 3:29.**

Took their lamps

The lamp is a symbol for the Word of God. **Psalm 119:105** All these virgins took with them a copy of the Word of God. Anybody can purchase a copy of the Word of God, but only those who apply Its teaching of salvation in the Lord Jesus Christ to their lives will have the indwelling Holy Spirit.

Bridegroom

The Hebrew wedding was a lot different than what we are used to in our twenty-first-century Western culture. The wedding ceremony was a long, drawn-out process. It began with a potential groom asking permission from a father to marry his daughter. If this was agreeable, they would have a wedding cup ceremony, in which the future bride would share a cup of wine with the groom to show her willingness to marry him. The groom would then have about a year to build a home for his new family. The home would have to be inspected by the father of the bride. The father of the bride had to approve of the new home before the wedding ceremony could take place. When all was ready, the groom would go to the home of the bride; take her from her father's home; take her to a private ceremony which would include the bride, the groom and the rabbi who performed the ceremony; then the couple would make a processional through the town calling all family and friends to join in the celebration. It was a parade through the town, culminating in a wedding feast at a predetermined location—the Marriage Supper. A company would be formed of those ready and willing to meet the Groom and Bride. **Luke 12:35-36**

And five of them were wise, and five *were* foolish.
[Matthew 25:2]

Five were foolish

The Greek word for foolish here is *moros*. It is the word from which we get the word "moron" in English. It does NOT mean to be ignorant. To be ignorant just means that there is something you do not know. NOBODY knows everything about everything, so all of us are ignorant about some things. It is not a problem to be ignorant. But it IS a problem to be foolish. It means to be stupid. To be foolish is to reject some knowledge from somebody who knows more than you in that subject. In this context, the foolish virgins were foolish because they were unprepared for the Messiah's Coming. To be unprepared for Messiah is just plain stupid. They had been given all the signs by the Lord Jesus Himself in the previous Chapter. They were given a VERY clear sign of the Abomination of Desolation. **Matthew 24:15**. When the nation of Israel saw THAT sign, they could start a one thousand two hundred sixty-day countdown until the Return of the Messiah. **Revelation 11:13; Revelation 12:6** They could have started a countdown on the calendar from the Antichrist's Abomination to the Messiah's Coming. But they rejected the Word of God. When you reject the Truth, the only thing left to believe is a lie. If you do not believe the Word of God, the Bible calls you a fool. **Psalm 14:1** These foolish virgins were stupid ONLY because they did NOT believe in the Word of God. That is why they were unprepared for the Messiah's Coming. They did NOT believe His Word.

> **They that *were* foolish took their lamps, and took no oil with them:**
>
> **[Matthew 25:3]**

Took no oil with them

In the Bible, oil is a symbol of the Holy Spirit. The Lord Jesus' Jewish hearers would have understood this symbolism from **Zechariah 4:6.** Note that the Word of God does NOT say that the foolish virgins RAN OUT of oil. It says that they HAD NO OIL. **Romans 8:9** tells us

> **…if any man have not the Spirit of Christ, he is none of His.**

All ten virgins had lamps. All ten set out to meet the Bridegroom. All ten fell asleep. The difference in the five wise and the five foolish virgins was a supply of oil. The wise had oil in their vessels. The foolish did not have any oil in their vessels. The lack of the Holy Spirit is a fatal flaw in all professors. They were NEVER really saved at all.

> **But the wise took oil in their vessels with their lamps.**
>
> **[Matthew 25:4]**

In their vessels

A vessel in the Scripture represents an individual's life. **Psalm 31:12; Acts 9:15; 1 Peter 3:7** For a believer, Paul says in **2 Corinthians 4:7** that we have this treasure in earthen vessels.

With their lamps

The lamps symbolize the Word of God. **Psalm 119:105** says

> **Thy word *is* a lamp unto my feet, and a light unto my path.**

Each virgin has a lamp. The Word of God illumines the darkness for ALL who use It. It is only through the convicting power of the Holy Spirit that the Word of God casts Its Light for salvation. **1 Corinthians 2:14** Each virgin has the initial convicting power of the Word. Some follow up that conviction by yielding to the Holy Spirit, and accepting the salvation that is offered in Christ.

> **While the bridegroom tarried, they all slumbered and slept.**
>
> [Matthew 25:5]

While the bridegroom tarried

All ten virgins stopped looking for the Bridegroom. The first-century Jewish believers that started the church were excited about the Second Coming of Christ. Paul himself looked to be alive when the Lord Jesus came back, and thought to be included in the Rapture. In **1 Thessalonians 4:15,** Paul uses the pronoun **we** to show that he thought he would be a part of it. However, the Lord Jesus did not come in the first century. The church gave up her Blessed Hope. It began to look to the things of the world, rather than the Coming of the Lord Jesus from Heaven. The church today has become more preoccupied with the things of the world rather than the Great Commission.

They all slumbered and slept

All ten virgins start out with lamps. Their lamps go out with the delay of the wedding procession. The lamps go out through the neglect of the virgins. ALL of us grow weary in the work of the Lord at times. Peter, James and John fell asleep at some crucial times in their ministries. In **Luke 9:32,** they fell asleep at the Mount of Transfiguration. Here were Moses, Elijah, and the Lord Jesus Christ—the greatest Bible conference of all time—and the disciples fell asleep. (That's why it no longer bothers me when people fall asleep when I preach. If they fell asleep on Moses, Elijah, and the Lord Jesus, they will fall asleep on me, too!) They also fell asleep in the Garden of Gethsemane the night the Lord Jesus was betrayed. **Matthew 26:40-41** But in the parable, five HAVE the Holy Spirit, and five DO NOT. Outwardly, they all look the same. Inwardly, they are different. The foolish never said, "yes" when the Holy Spirit was convicting them to believe in the Coming King. Believers are warned to keep a watch, and not grow weary in our service for the Lord. Awake from sleep and get busy for the Lord! **Romans 13:11; 1 Thessalonians 5:6**

> **And at midnight there was a cry made, Behold, the bridegroom cometh; go ye out to meet him.**
> **[Matthew 25:6]**

At midnight

At midnight, all the sleepers were awakened. There was some quickening of end-times events that shook them from their slumber. It was a clarion call of God. Perhaps it was the appearance of the Shekinah Glory of God from **Matthew 24:30.** Maybe it was the call of the Trumpet gathering the believing remnant of Israel from **Matthew 24:31.** We are not told WHAT woke the sleepers, but whatever it was, the call was unmistakable. "The time has come! The Messiah is here at last!"

Cry

The Midnight Cry revealed the true condition of the hearts of these virgins. It is the heart that will be exposed. **Matthew 24:48** The Midnight Cry will expose the heart, and separate the professors from the possessors.

> **Then all those virgins arose, and trimmed their lamps.**
>
> **[Matthew 25:7]**

Trimmed their lamps

The current teaching of our day states that man will have a chance after death to accept the Lord Jesus Christ as Saviour. Many point to this verse to show that all the virgins got ready after the Midnight Cry. However, we note that at the trimming of the lamps, five were unprepared. This is because they had no oil. The five foolish virgins appeared to be getting ready. They were trimming their lamps. To the outside world, they were preparing to meet the Bridegroom. However, they had no oil. They could not get their vessels to shine because they had no oil. They were NOT given a second chance, because they were unprepared when they heard the Midnight Cry.

> **And the foolish said unto the wise, Give us of your oil; for our lamps are gone out.**
> **[Matthew 25:8]**

The foolish said

The foolish virgins are awakened and discover their tragic mistake. They have no oil. They do not have the Holy Spirit after all. They are not really saved at all.

The wise

The wise virgins are able to relight their lamps. They have oil. They follow the leading of the Holy Spirit, and are ready to meet the Bridegroom. They have believed the Word of God, and are truly saved.

Give us

The Holy Spirit cannot be shared. You cannot get to Heaven on the strength of somebody else's spiritual experience. God has no grandchildren. Salvation MUST be a personal, individual matter between you and God alone.

> **But the wise answered, saying, *Not so*; lest there be not enough for us and you: but go ye rather to them that sell, and buy for yourselves.**
>
> **[Matthew 25:9]**

Go ye rather to them that sell

The foolish virgins have waited until it was too late. Notice that the Scripture text never says that these foolish virgins ever found any oil. They just stumbled in the darkness in a vain attempt to find the Holy Spirit of God. Where could they go now? The two fiery evangelists have been put to death and taken into Heaven. **Revelation 11:7-12** The 144,000 Jewish evangelists have already heard the Midnight Cry, and are already seated at the Marriage Supper. **Revelation 14:1** There was no place for the foolish to turn to now. It reminds us of the solemn warning of the Lord Jesus to Nicodemus in **John 3:8.** The Lord Jesus likened the conviction of the Holy Spirit to the wind. He told Nicodemus that you could feel the wind, you could see the effects of the wind, but you cannot control the wind. So while the wind is blowing, you had better take advantage of it. The Holy Spirit is the same way. Many have felt the convicting power of the Holy Spirit, but have not heeded His call to salvation. You had better take advantage of His convicting power while you can, because He may not come around to call you to salvation again. There was no buying oil now. These foolish virgins missed the call to come and buy without money and without price. **Isaiah 55:1-3** It was too late now.

> **And while they went to buy, the bridegroom came; and they that were ready went in with him to the marriage: and the door was shut.**
> **[Matthew 25:10]**

The Bridegroom came

While the foolish virgins were stumbling in the darkness seeking in vain for oil, the Bridegroom arrived.

They that were ready

To be ready is to be a believer. You must believe in God's Word. You must believe in God's Messiah. The Lord Jesus warns over and over in this sermon—BE READY!!! Note that only those who were ready were allowed to go into the Marriage Supper with the Bridegroom.

Door

The Lord Jesus Himself is the Door. **John 10:9**

> **I am the door: by me if any man enter in, he shall be saved, and shall go in and out, and find pasture.**

You cannot get into Heaven through the door of a Baptist Church. You cannot get into Heaven through the door of a Catholic Church, or Methodist Church, or Presbyterian Church. The ONLY Door into Heaven is the Lord Jesus Christ Himself.

Shut

These are ominous words from the Lips of the Lord Jesus. When the Lord shuts the door, NO MAN will be able to open it. **Isaiah 22:22; Luke 13:25; Revelation 3:7** The LORD Himself closed the door to Noah's ark, and no power on Earth could open it again. **Genesis 7:16** Midnight brought a cry. Now the foolish virgins face the dawning of a new day—an Eternal Day shut off from Christ for all eternity.

> **Afterward came also the other virgins, saying, Lord, Lord, open to us.**
> **[Matthew 25:11]**

Afterward

This is a solemn word. To be in the afterward crowd means that you have missed the opportunity to be saved. These ten foolish virgins thought they had all the time in the world. But when the Midnight Cry came, they were unprepared. It was eternally too late for them. They should have come to believe in the Word of God while there was yet time. What about you?

> **But he answered and said, Verily I say unto you, I know you not.**
>
> **[Matthew 25:12]**

Verily

This word means "truthfully." You can almost hear the tinge of sadness in the Voice of the Lord Jesus as He speaks. A wedding feast is no place for strangers. Only friends and family are invited to attend. All others are unknown by the wedding party, and are excluded from the festivities.

I know ye not

The foolish virgins had the language of a believer, but not the life of a believer. They had religion, but did not have Christ. They had the Word of God, but not the Spirit of God. No doubt they could quote Scripture, spout doctrine, answer all the catechisms. But they had no personal relationship with the Messiah King. The door has been shut. They are on the wrong side. They call His Name, but He does not know them. They will hear the frightful words from **Matthew 7:21-23,**

> **Not every one that saith unto me, Lord, Lord, shall enter into the Kingdom of Heaven; but he**

that doeth the will of my Father which is in Heaven. Many will say unto Me in that day, Lord, Lord, have we not prophesied in Thy Name? And in Thy Name cast out devils? And in Thy Name done many wonderful works? And then will I profess unto them, I never knew you: depart from me, ye that work iniquity.

Watch therefore, for ye know neither the day nor the hour wherein the Son of man cometh.
[Matthew 25:13]

Watch therefore

This parable ends with a familiar warning. **Watch** ... This applies to all those of the nation of Israel that are left after the Rapture. They will be living in a world dominated by Satan and his man, the Antichrist. The power of Satan will be strong in those days. It will be so strong that he will ALMOST be able to fool God's elect. **Matthew 24:24** This is a warning to the remnant of Israel in those days NOT to neglect the possession of Divine Light from the Scriptures. They must be sure to answer the call of God to believe in His Word, and in His Messiah. Many will be aroused by the Rapture of the church in the beginning of the Tribulation. There will be a new spiritual excitement and awakening as the two witnesses and the 144,000 Jewish evangelists proclaim the Gospel of the Coming Kingdom. There will be MANY who feel that conviction, but neglect the all-important step of personally believing in the Coming King. They will be dead to the signs that the King Himself gave them in this prophetic sermon on top of the Mount of Olives. They have rejected the Word of God. They will turn away from the Light of God's Word. They will be lost for all eternity. Where will YOU be for eternity?

CHAPTER SIX

THE PARABLE OF THE TALENTS

MATTHEW 25:14-30

This is the third and final parable the Lord Jesus uses to illustrate His great prophetic sermon—the Olivet Discourse. After this, the Lord Jesus has one final word of prophecy, and His sermon on the end times will be complete. This parable discusses a nobleman's departure and return. It represents a period between the Lord's Ascension and Second Coming. The parable is meant to teach accountability. It applies to ALL believers who are living while the Lord Jesus is away. It concerns two days—a day of responsibility, and a day of accountability.

> For *the kingdom of heaven is* as a man travelling into a far country, *who* called his own servants, and delivered unto them his goods.
>
> [Matthew 25:14]

Far country

The Lord Jesus was in the nation of Israel some two thousand years ago. He presented Himself as the long-awaited Messiah and King, but He was rejected by His own people. **John 1:11** He left the nation of Israel and left for the far country of Heaven. **Mark 16:19; Luke 19:12** He is in Heaven now presiding over a different Body than was promised to Israel through the Old Testament prophets. He presides now over the Church. He will return to Israel one day to rebuild the Tabernacle of David, as James preached in **Acts 15:14-17**. He will do so and fulfill all His promises and prophecies to the nation of Israel during the Millennial Kingdom.

His own servants

The Lord Jesus uses this term for the believing remnant of Israel in the last days. He calls believers in the Church His friends. **John 15:15**

> **And unto one he gave five talents, to another two, and to another one; to every man according to his several ability; and straightway took his journey.**
> **[Matthew 25:15]**

Talents

A talent in the days in which the Lord Jesus was preaching was a silver coin (or sum of money) weighing somewhere between seventy-five and a hundred pounds. It was the largest known measure of wealth, merchandise or economics in the Roman period. The talent was worth 10,000 denarii. A denarius was a day's wage for a common laborer. A common laborer would have to work every day, seven days a week, without a day off for nearly twenty-eight straight years in order to earn a talent. It was a fortune! It represented a lifetime's work for the common man. These servants were entrusted with a great responsibility.

To every man according to his several ability

This shows the Sovereign wisdom of God. God gives as HE sees fit. **1 Corinthians 12:11; Ephesians 4:16** He will never put on us more than we can bear in our service for Him. **1 Corinthians 10:13** The goal of EVERY spiritual gift is to glorify Him—not to glorify the steward of God's gift. Each servant is entrusted with a great responsibility. They will have to stand true in the days when Antichrist is wreaking havoc of the believing remnant of Israel, and try to share the Gospel of the Kingdom when it could cost them their lives.

> **Then he that had received the five talents went and traded with the same, and made *them* other five talents.**
>
> [**Matthew 25:16**]

Went and traded

Two of the three servants went to work immediately. The third went and hid his talent. The Master knew the hearts of these servants. He knew that even the third servant had SOME ability. Even one talent was a fortune. He had no excuse for burying his talent. The third servant became unprofitable simply by doing nothing.

And made then other five talents

The first servant was given five talents, which was according to his several ability in his Mater's Eyes. His faithfulness gained a one hundred percent return on his Master's investment. Faithfulness for the Lord Jesus ALWAYS pays off in the end.

> **And likewise he that *had received* two, he also gained other two.**
> **[Matthew 25:17]**

He also gained other two

Like the first servant, this one was also faithful. He likewise received a one hundred percent return on his Master's investment.

> **But he that had received one went and digged in the earth, and hid his lord's money.**
> **[Matthew 25:18]**

Hid his lord's money

This servant was not faithful at all. The reason

he was not faithful was because he really did not be-lieve his Master's Word that he would return. Many of the remnant of Israel will miss the Coming of the King because they will refuse to believe His Word.

After a long time the lord of those servants co-meth, and reckoneth with them.
                                        [Matthew 25:19]

After a long time

This is the only time in the entire Word of God where the Lord Jesus gives even the slightest hint that there may be a delay between His Ascension and Second Coming.

The lord of those servants cometh

Even though there may be a delay between His two Comings, we can be one hundred percent as-sured that His Second Coming will take place. It will be an actual, historical event on planet Earth. His Second Coming is as sure as the Word of God, which the Lord Jesus said was to stand forever. **Matthew 24:35** When He left for the far country, He gave His disciples the promise that He would return some day. **Acts 1:9-11**

And reckoneth with them

The word **reckoneth** means "to be called into

account." These servants were given instructions to **Occupy till I come. Luke 19:13** The time for stewardship has past. Now each servant faces a time of reckoning.

> And so he that had received five talents came and brought other five talents, saying, Lord, thou deliveredst unto me five talents: behold, I have gained beside them five talents more.
>
> [Matthew 25:20]

Behold, I have gained five talents more

This shows that spiritual gifts can be expanded. Two of these servants traded with the Lord's talents and doubled them. **Luke 19:15** Exercise of any spiritual gift will strengthen and enlarge it. The results will be a net gain for the Lord Jesus. The more a believer witnesses, the more will hear the Gospel, and the more will become converted.

> His lord said unto him, Well done, *thou* good and faithful servant: thou hast been faithful over a few things, I will make thee ruler over many things: enter thou into the joy of thy lord.
>
> [Matthew 25:21]

Well done

Notice that each of these two servants receives the same reward. The one who gained five talents is not put on a pedestal, nor does he receive a greater reward than the one who gained the two talents. Both are commended equally. This is a verse I will always associate with my beloved Pastor David Ray. He was a true servant of God. All he ever wanted for his 33 years of service for the Lord Jesus was to hear Him say these Words to him in Glory one day—

> **...Well done, *thou* good and faithful servant... enter into the joy of thy Lord.**

In a day of religious charlatans and money-making gimmicks of televangelists, it is refreshing and inspiring to find such a servant of God still around in the work of the Lord Jesus today.

Thou hast been faithful

Notice that the Lord Jesus does NOT say, "Well done thou good and PROFITABLE servant." Nor does He say, "Well done thou good and SUCCESS-FUL servant." There is no question of bigness, greatness, profit or success in the eyes of the world. The only thing that matters to the Master is FAITH-FULNESS. **1 Corinthians 4:5; 1 Peter 1:7; Philippians 3:14; 1 John 2:28; 2 Peter 1:11; Luke 19:17** The Lord is concerned with faithfulness of all His servants. **1 Corinthians 4:2** tells us

Moreover it is required in stewards, that a man be found faithful.

A servant who is faithful to his master shows that his heart is right between him and his Lord. **John 14:15** Paul knew that feeling, and rejoiced in it before he left this Earth. **2 Timothy 4:7** Norbert Lieth wrote of a story that illustrates this Biblical Truth. An elderly blind woman had a French Bible, and asked one of her grandsons to underline **Jean 3:16** in it. Not understanding why his blind grandmother would want a Bible passage underlined, he accommodated her. She took her French Bible and would sit in a bench outside a school to wait for the children to leave for the day. She would ask some children if they had paid attention to their French lessons. If they said they had, she would ask them to read the underlined passage in her French Bible. That opened the door to witness for her Lord. Several of these children were saved through her ministry over the years, and twenty-four of them became preachers and missionaries. She did what she COULD. She was faithful.

Ruler over many things

The two faithful servants started out as servants. They were later promoted to rulers. This was the highest possible reward for those of Israel who re-

main true to the King during the Tribulation period. They will live and reign with Christ for one
thousand years. **Revelation 20:4**

> **He also that had received two talents came and
> said, Lord, thou deliveredst unto me two talents:
> behold, I have gained two other talents beside
> them.**
>
> **[Matthew 25:22]**

I have gained two other talents beside them

At the time of reckoning, this steward was not
ashamed. He had been doing what he had been
instructed to do while his Lord was away. He had
been faithful to his Master's word. When we have
been faithful to the Word of God, we will have nothing to be ashamed of when we face the Lord Jesus at
the Judgment Seat of Christ.

> **His lord said unto him, Well done, good and
> faithful servant; thou hast been faithful over
> a few things, I will make thee ruler over many
> things: enter thou into the joy of thy lord.**
>
> **[Matthew 25:23]**

Enter thou into the joy of thy lord

This servant also received the reward of being
with his Lord for all eternity. That reward awaits all
true believers of all ages.

> Then he which had received the one talent came
> and said, Lord, I knew thee that thou art an hard
> man, reaping where thou hast not sown, and
> gathering where thou hast not strawed:
>
> [Matthew 25:24]

Then he which had received the one talent came and said

The wicked servant was never a believer in his Master at all. His own testimony condemns him as an unbeliever. His very words show what evil is in his heart. **Matthew 15:19**

I know thee

He blames God for his own sin. He is telling his Lord that he knows that he can do nothing to please his Master, who expects unreasonable things from His servants. He is accusing his Master of never being satisfied. He says that his Master cannot be pleased with anything. Of course, this is a lie. He already was satisfied with the other two servants who traded wisely with their entrusted amounts. But it has always been so. Ever since the Garden of Eden, man has been blaming God for his own sin. Adam blamed God for giving him the woman. **Genesis 3:12** God will forgive EVERY confessed sin, **1 John 1:9,** but He will never forgive an excuse. In order to be forgiven, a person must stop making lame excuses, admit his sin, and ask God for forgiveness of his sin through the Blood of Jesus Christ.

Thou art an hard man

This servant called his Master "fierce." It is the same language used of the Egyptian taskmasters of the Hebrew slaves in **Exodus 1:11.** Yet it was the LORD that relieved the Hebrews of their servitude. He was not the One Who put them under bondage, but He was the One Who delivered the nation of Israel through power and blood. His very words show that he does not know Who his Master at all.

Reaping where thou hast not sown

The wicked servant accuses his Master of dishonesty and unfairness. Millions today still accuse God of being unfair. After all, His way of doing things does not measure up to the way THEY think things should be done. It is a fulfillment of **Isaiah 55:8.** People still blame God for their own sins everyday. They say things that sound reasonable to them. They say things like, "If there is a loving God, He won't send anybody to Hell," or "It doesn't matter what you believe, as long as you're sincere," or thousands of other little sayings that make sense to the modern man. The only problem with this thinking is that they are all one hundred percent contradictory to the Word of God. In a small manner, they are slightly correct. In fact, God is NOT fair with man. "Fair" means getting exactly what we deserve. "Fair" does NOT mean things should happen the way I think they should happen. If God were truly fair with man, every one of us would have been in hell years ago. But God does not want to deal with man in fairness. He wants to deal with man in grace. "Grace" is getting what we do not deserve. We do not deserve salvation through the death of God on the Cross, but God has ordained this plan the ONLY way of salvation. **John 14:6; Acts 4:12** God wants to deal with you in grace, but if you demand a fair trial, God will deal with you in judgment. If you want what is fair, it will land you in the Lake of Fire for all eternity, because **all have sinned and come short of the Glory of God. Romans 3:23**

> **And I was afraid, and went and hid thy talent in the earth: lo, *there* thou hast *that* is thine.**
>   **[Matthew 25:25]**

I was afraid

This shows the conviction of the wicked servant's heart. He has no confidence or peace in his heart. **Romans 5:1** tells us that the Lord Jesus came to bring peace to the human heart. He died on the Cross to make peace between man and God. This man is still at war with God. He is afraid. He has no peace in his heart. He does not trust in the Lord at all.

Hid thy talent in the earth

This shows that this wicked servant is a mere professor. He had no faith in his Master's promise to return. He did not believe in the Word of his Master. He wanted to be wise in the eyes of the world. He wanted to play both ends against the middle. He wanted to play every angle in order to make sure that everything worked out to HIS advantage, not his Lord's gain. He probably reasoned thusly: "I do not believe that my Master will return as He said. I will bury this fortune in a place where nobody will be able to find it. That way, when he does not return, this fortune will be all mine. If I give it to the bankers to draw interest for my Master, I will have to register it in His name, and it will become a part of his estate. I will never see a penny of it. If He does not return, I can simply dig it up, and enjoy the privileges that come with wealth. However, if He does return, I can always dig it up again, present it to Him, and never be accused of being a thief, since he will receive every penny of His money. Nobody will be the wiser, and I may become the richer." This thinking showed careful calculation on the part of this wicked servant. The world would applaud this man for his clear thinking. However, this man was NOT judged by the world. This thinking also shows clear premeditation. He would be convicted in any court of law in the land. But most of all, this thinking shows what was in his heart. His heart was full of avarice, greed and envy for his Master's money. He cared more about the rewards of service than service for the Master Himself. This shows that he was a mere professor, and not a possessor.

There thou hast that is thine

His excuse is self-incriminating. He admits that he knows and understands that this money was never his in the first place. He admits that he would have never touched this money if his Lord had not entrusted him with it in the first place. It is NOT his money at all. It came from the Lord. He had no right to it.

> His lord answered and said unto him, *Thou* wicked and slothful servant, thou knewest that I reap where I sowed not, and gather where I have not strawed:
>
> [Matthew 25:26]

Thou wicked

The word wicked is literally "evil." It is used of the lost in the Old Testament. **Genesis 18:25; Ecclesiastes 8:13; Isaiah 53:9** This shows that this man is not a believer in his Master at all. It is wicked to be disobedient to the Word of God. It is wicked

not to believe in the Word of God. He does not believe in the Word of God, so he has no desire to seek
the Word of God.

Slothful servant

The word slothful means "lazy." It means to be
idle by choice when there is work to be done. It
means to choose to lay in bed when it is time to
work. He was not guilty of some gross sin in the eyes
of the world. This servant was no murderer; not an
adulterer; not a drunkard. But he WAS guilty of the
only sin that will send a soul to hell. He did not believe in the Word of God. He rejected his Master's
offer of eternal salvation because he chose not to
take God at His Word.

> **Thou oughtest therefore to have put my money to
> the exchangers, and *then* at my coming I should
> have received mine own with usury.**
> **[Matthew 25:27]**

Put my money to the exchangers

This servant really had no excuse. His mouth has
been stopped. **Romans 3:19** All unbelievers' petty
little excuses will melt away before the Throne of
the Universe.

I should have received mine own with usury

The steward at least could have given his master's talent to the bank, and let it draw interest. Even that small amount would have shown some faithfulness of the servant's part. **Luke 19:23**

> **Take therefore the talent from him, and give *it* unto him which hath ten talents.**
> **[Matthew 25:28]**

Give it unto him which hath ten talents

ALL faithful service for the Master will be rewarded. **Luke 19:25**

> **For unto every one that hath shall be given, and he shall have abundance: but from him that hath not shall be taken away even that which he hath.**
> **[Matthew 25:29]**

He shall have abundance

Faithful service for the Master results in a reward of His blessings. Those rewards are not always realized on Earth, despite what the prosperity gospel preaches may say. However, the rewards the faithful will receive will last for all eternity. Faithful servants will be in the presence of the Lord Jesus Christ for all eternity.

Shall be taken away even that which he hath

God will never reward faithlessness. In fact, it will be punished by taking away of what could have been a reward. **Mark 4:25; Luke 19:26**

> **And cast ye the unprofitable servant into outer darkness: there shall be weeping and gnashing of teeth.**
>
> **[Matthew 25:30]**

There shall be weeping and gnashing of teeth

The language used here by the Lord Jesus is elsewhere used in the Word of God to describe the conditions and torments of hell. **Psalm 112:10; Matthew 8:12; Matthew 13:42; Matthew 22:13; Matthew 24:51; Luke 13:28; Jude 1:13** The only other places this language is used is in connection with the lost. This shows that this wicked servant was never saved in the first place.

For the child of God, this parable has two applications. 1) Find out what God wants you to do. 2) Be faithful to do it. To some, God gives a very small ministry. That may be upsetting to us, but if God makes you a one-talent servant, He has still entrusted you with a fortune! Be faithful to what He has given you to do. That's all He asks. Only eternity will tell the story. It may well be that an unseen faithful grandmother who prayed faithfully for her family will receive a greater reward in Glory than a world-famous evangelist that was not faithful to what God gave him. However, for the unbeliever, there is only ONE application. That is to believe the Word of God, and accept the salvation He offers through the shed Blood of His Son Jesus Christ on the Cross of Calvary.

CHAPTER SEVEN

THE JUDGMENT OF THE SHEEP AND THE GOATS

MATTHEW 25:31-46

The Lord Jesus ends His important, prophetic Olivet Discourse with this final prophecy. Many have abused this passage. They call it a parable. Liberal theologians have used this so-called parable to give justification for their social gospel. There is no parabolic language in this prophetic passage. There is no statement from the Lips of the Saviour that gives any indication of this passage being a parable. He does NOT begin by likening the Kingdom of Heaven to some Earthly correlation, as He did in the previous parables. In **Matthew 25:1**, the Lord Jesus begins by saying, **then shall the Kingdom of Heaven be likened unto** ... There is no such parabolic language in this part of the Olivet Discourse. This is a prophecy. As we study this passage, we must remember the context. The Times of the Gentiles **(Luke 21:24)** has run its course. It started in 586 BC with the Babylonian conquest of Jerusalem under the hand of Nebuchadnezzar, and ended at the Battle of Armageddon with the Second Coming of Christ to close the Great Tribulation Period. During the Times of the Gentiles, the leaders of the world have attempted to exterminate the Jewish race from off the face of the Earth. Now, the tables have turned. Under the Messiah, Israel has become the head of the nations, and not the tail. **Deuteronomy 28:13** In this passage, the Lord Jesus refers to Himself as King for the only time in His Earthly ministry. Immediately after preaching this sermon, He would accept a crown. But it would not be the crown He speaks of here. He would go on to be crowned with a crown of thorns by a mocking, Christ-rejecting world. The Cross would only be three days away.

> **When the Son of man shall come in his glory, and all the holy angels with him, then shall he sit upon the throne of his glory.**
>
> **[Matthew 25:31]**

When the Son of man shall come in His Glory

This shows the timing of this prophetic scene. The Battle of Armageddon has already taken place. The Great Tribulation is over. What is left of the human race is summoned to the Valley of Jehoshaphat near Jerusalem to be judged. This was foretold in **Joel 3:2-12; Zechariah 14:4**. We must remember that less than half of the population of the Earth that enters the seven-year period of the Tribulation will survive until the end. Wars, pestilences, famines, "natural" catastrophes, the judgments of God, and the bloody reign of the Beast will destroy more than half the world's population. **Revelation 6-18** The survivors are summoned to the Judgment of the Nations.

All the holy angels with Him

The Lord Jesus told the disciples that His angels will be ministers of judgment in the Parable of the Wheat and the Tares in **Matthew 13:41**, and also in **Matthew 24:31**. Here, we see the fulfillment of that parable as the angels help the Lord Jesus separate the wheat from the tares at His Second Coming.

Then shall He sit upon the throne of His Glory

Many have "spiritualized" this Throne to mean to believer's heart. That is clearly not what the Lord Jesus intended here, and would not have been clearly understood by the disciples that asked the questions that started this sermon in the first place. The Jewish disciples would have understood this promise in the light of Old Testament prophecy of the literal, governmental Throne of the Messiah during the Millennial Reign of the Messiah for one thousand years. **Daniel 7:14; Matthew 19:28; 1 Thes-**

salonians 1:10 In fact, the Messiah's Throne is the theme and culmination of ALL the prophecies and promises in the Old Testament to Israel. It was promised in the great Davidic Covenant in **2 Samuel 7:13; 1 Chronicles 17:12;** and **Psalm 2:6.** It was the Throne promised at the Annunciation to the Virgin Mary by the Heavenly messenger Gabriel. **Luke 1:32** It was the Throne the Lord Jesus Himself promised to the disciple Peter in **Matthew 19:28**. In that passage, the Lord Jesus even used the same phrase—the Throne of His Glory. This Throne will be the governmental AND religious center of the Earth for one thousand years. The first thing the King does when He comes again is set up His Throne. It is a Throne of Judgment. **Psalm 9:7; Psalm 72:2; Psalm 75:2; Psalm 110:6**

His Glory

This phrase is used twice in this verse that opens the final portion of the Olivet Discourse. In the Jewish though and mindset, this would refer to the Shekinah Glory of God, which was the visible Presence of God Himself among His people. The Lord Jesus used this phrase twice in this verse to remind His Jewish disciples that when He comes again, His Glory will be unveiled and revealed for all the world to see. He will dwell among his people as God and as King! His reign will be the culmination of all the

Old Testament Prophetic Word of God to the nation of Israel.

> **And before him shall be gathered all nations: and he shall separate them one from another, as a shepherd divideth *his* sheep from the goats.**
> **[Matthew 25:32]**

Before Him shall be gathered

This gathering of the nations before the Judge was foretold in **Joel 2:11-16; Psalm 50:5; John 5:22; Jude 1:15; Ezekiel 34:20; Revelation 20:5; Obadiah 1:15; Numbers 23:9** and in **Zechariah 14:1-5.** There are three distinct groups that appear before the Throne. There are the sheep, the goats, and My brethren **(Matthew 25:40)**. The brethren to which the Lord Jesus refers are the survivors of the Hebrew nation of Israel. They are His kinsmen according to the flesh. **Deuteronomy 17:15; Romans 9:3**

All nations

The Gospel of the Kingdom was preached into ALL the world. **Matthew 24:14** ALL people of the world had the opportunity to accept or reject the message of the soon-Coming King. Nations here is the Greek word *ethne*. It is elsewhere translated "Gentiles." It shows ethnicity. It shows that there are different peoples, languages, religions, and cultures that stand before the King. The Jewish nation is NOT included in this judgment. **Numbers 23:9** says that Israel shall not be reckoned among the nations. The nation of Israel was a special work of God for the salvation of the human race. It began with the call of Abraham in **Genesis 12:1-3.** Also, all surviving Israelites will be saved on the Day when the Messiah King returns to planet Earth. **Isaiah 66:8; Romans 11:26** Israel will stand with the King. The Gentile nations here do not include the Church either. The Church will come with the King. **Jude 1:14; 1 Thessalonians 3:13**

Separate them one from another

The Word of God tells us that ALL future judgment is committed to the Lord Jesus Christ. **John 5:22** He is the ONLY One Who ever lived that qualifies to judge others, because He is the Only One Who did the will of God the Father one hundred percent while He was here on Earth. **John 8:29** This is NOT the Great White Throne Judgment of **Revelation 20:11-15.** These two judgments are separated by one thousand years of human history. Liberal theologians have merged these two judgments into one, and called it a "general judgment." The concept of a general judgment is found nowhere in Scripture. Liberal theologians have done the same with the two resurrections. They merge them and call them the "general resurrection." But the Word of God clearly teaches that there will be a resurrection of the just, and a resurrection of the lost. **Daniel 12:2; John 5:29**

> **And he shall set the sheep on his right hand, but the goats on the left.**
>
> [**Matthew 25:33**]

He shall set the sheep on his right hand

We must remember the background of this judgment. The world has just gone through the Great Tribulation. For three and a half years, the Beast has been on a bloody quest to eliminate all those who believe in the Coming King. Those especially target for attack are the Jewish people. **Revelation 12:17** Here and there, a few Gentiles offer some kind of assistance to a fleeing Jew. The sheep are few and far between. Most people on Earth will fall into step with the program of the Beast's final holocaust of the Jewish race. However, the Lord Jesus has already promised that the generation of Jewish people would never be destroyed from the face of the Earth before Messiah Comes Again. **Matthew 24:34** Here, He makes sure He keeps His promise to His brethren. The criterion of this judgment is only one question—"What did you do for My brethren?" This question goes straight to the heart. The root of the criterion is anti-Semitism. The survivors are gathered to the Valley of Jehoshaphat. The nightmare is over! The Messiah is here! Three thousand five hundred years of God's promises and prophecies to the nation of Israel are about to be fulfilled in the Person of the long-awaited Messiah. A group of unbelieving Gentiles have outlived Satan's superman, the Beast. Most of these gathered are branded with his damning mark. **Revelation 13:16-17** Now, they look upon the One whom they pierced. **John 19:37**

> **Then shall the King say unto them on his right hand, Come, ye blessed of my Father, inherit the kingdom prepared for you from the foundation of the world:**
>
> **[Matthew 25:34]**

Unto them on his right hand

The Valley of Jehoshaphat lies between the city of Jerusalem and the Mount of Olives. The Garden of Gethsemane lies at the foot of the Mount of Olives facing the Holy City. At the Judgment of the Nations, the sheep stand at the Lord Jesus' Right Hand. They are placed toward Jerusalem, the City of the Great King. **Psalm 48:2; Matthew 5:35** The goats are placed on the King's Left Hand. They are placed close to the Valley of Gehenna, or the Valley of Himmon. That was the eternally-burning garbage dump outside the city limits of Jerusalem. The Lord Jesus used this garbage dump as an illustration of the eternal fire of hell many times in Scripture. All those who come to the Lord Jesus are promised eternal rest. **Matthew 11:28**

Come

These Gentiles will enter into the Millennial Kingdom of the Messiah. As righteous, they will later go into Eternal Life. Their belief in the King means that they will not follow Satan in his final rebellion. **Revelation 20:7-10 Come** is the great invitation of the Word of God. It was first used with Noah in **Genesis 7:1**. The LORD God invited Noah to come into the ark. He did not tell Noah to GO into the ark, but to come. The reason for this was that God was already in the ark. God never asks us to go anyplace where He is not already there waiting for us. The very last page of the Word of God gives this same great invitation. As God closes His Word forever, He issues one last invitation for man to come to Him. **Revelation 22:17** The Lord Jesus used this great invitation in His Earthly ministry. In **Matthew 11:28,** the Lord Jesus said,

> **Come unto me, all ye that labour and are heavy laden, and I will give you rest.**

The invitation goes out still today for ALL men to come to salvation in Christ. There will be a day when the invitation is no longer given. Do not wait until it is everlastingly too late to try to come to Jesus the Saviour.

Blessed of my Father

This fulfills the prophecy and promise of the Abrahamic Covenant of **Genesis 12:3**. God promised Abraham that He would bless them that bless thee. God always keeps His promises. God cannot lie. **Titus 1:2** He promised Abraham, the father of the Hebrew nation, that He would bless all those who were a blessing to the nation of Israel. History has borne this out, but the ultimate fulfillment will be at the Judgment of the Nations. Because of their treatment of the Lord's brethren during the Tribulation Period, these Gentiles inherit the Millennial Kingdom that was prepared for them from the foundation of the world. **Luke 1:33; Revelation 20:4** This is a great inheritance for these believing, sheep Gentiles. We must remember that the Church's inheritance is MUCH greater than a Kingdom. Our inheritance is the King Himself. Our inheritance is Christ. **Ephesians 1:3** Through the Work of the Lord Jesus on the Cross, we have become joint-heirs in Christ. **Romans 8:17**

> For I was an hungered, and ye gave me meat: I was thirsty, and ye gave me drink: I was a stranger, and ye took me in:
>
> [Matthew 25:35]

I was an hungered

Many believing and evangelistic Jewish believers are to be tormented during the reign of antichrist. They have a promise form the Messiah-King that during His Reign, they shall hunger no more, nether thirst any more. **Revelation 7:16**

Ye gave me meat

During the time the Beast was ruling on Planet Earth, it cost something to be a friend of the Jewish people. By merely feeding the Earthly brothers of the Coming King, these Gentiles risked their own lives by assisting the Jewish people.

> Naked, and ye clothed me: I was sick, and ye visited me: I was in prison, and ye came unto me.
>
> [Matthew 25:36]

Ye came unto me

This was even a riskier proposition during the reign of the Antichrist. To visit a Jewish prisoner and attempt to give aid was to publicly risk arrest and imprisonment. Hospital or prison visitation to a Jew during the Tribulation Period meant a person was standing in direct, open opposition to the Beast. This work will be rewarded by the King in His Millennial Kingdom. **Hebrews 13:3**

> **Then shall the righteous answer him, saying, Lord, when saw we thee an hungered, and fed *thee*? or thirsty, and gave thee drink?**
>   **[Matthew 25:37]**

The righteous

These Gentile sheep are believers. They are NOT saved by works. Rather, their works on behalf of the Jews during the Tribulation Period are merely a manifestation of the faith in their hearts. In other words, their works SHOW their faith. **James 2:18** Their treatment of the Jews during the Tribulation Period shows their faith in the Coming King. They BELIEVED in the Gospel of the Kingdom, and they acted accordingly. Their actions revealed the belief that was already present in their hearts. **Hebrews 11:6**

When saw we Thee

This question from the heart shows that their hearts were right with the Lord. Their hearts were right because their motives were right. They were not being friendly to God's persecuted people for the sake of personal gain or reward. They were surprised by the Words of the Messiah-King inviting them into the Kingdom. It shows that they had a true, sacrificial, agape love for the Coming King and His people. The actions always reveal what is in the heart.

> **When saw we thee a stranger, and took thee in? or naked, and clothed *thee*?**
>
> **[Matthew 25:38]**

When saw we Thee

The believing Gentiles are perplexed. They never saw the KING hungry, thirsty, in hospital or prison.

> **Or when saw we thee sick, or in prison, and came unto thee?**
>
> **[Matthew 25:39]**

When saw we Thee

The believing Gentiles never did these things for the King Himself, but they did these things for the King's brethren according to the flesh. They did these things for the Jewish people during the Tribulation.

> **And the King shall answer and say unto them, Verily I say unto you, Inasmuch as ye have done *it* unto one of the least of these my brethren, ye have done *it* unto me.**
>
> **[Matthew 25:40]**

My brethren

The Lord Jesus calls the remnant of the nation of Israel My brethren. **Matthew 28:10** This phrase alone clearly expresses how God Himself really sees the Jewish people. There is NO place in the believer's life for ANY form of anti-Semitism whatsoever. To hate the Jewish people is to hate the Lord Jesus Himself.

Ye have done it

Again, these Gentiles are NOT saved by their works. Nobody in history has ever been saved because of their good works. Rather, the sheep's works show that they have already become believers in the Gospel of the Kingdom. **Matthew 24:14** They manifest their faith by their works. **James 2:14-21.** These are not works FOR salvation, they are works OF salvation. They are not saved because of their works, they work because they are saved. **James 2:26** reminds us that faith without works is dead. We see the fruit of their salvation. To clothe, feed, or befriend a Jew during the Great Tribulation is to invite certain wrath, even death by beheading at the hands of the Beast. **Revelation 20:4** These sheep literally have stuck their necks out to help the King's brethren during the time of unprecedented crisis.

Unto me

The Lord Jesus identifies Himself with the persecuted nation of Israel. **Matthew 10:40-42; Mark 9:41; Romans 9:4; Deuteronomy 17:15; Matthew 28:10; Joel 3:3** Israel is the apple of God's eye. **Zechariah 2:8** Every sin is ultimately a sin against God. Your behavior always reflects your faith. One of the criteria God uses to judge us is if we love our brothers and sisters in Christ. **1 John 2:9-11** This passage tells us that if you do not love your brother that you have seen, how can you love God Whom you have not seen?

> **Then shall he say also unto them on the left hand, Depart from me, ye cursed, into everlasting fire, prepared for the devil and his angels:**
> **[Matthew 25:41]**

Them on the left hand

Those on the King's Left Hand have no hope. They refused to believe in the Gospel of the Kingdom. They took the Mark of the Beast. **Revelation 13:16** They were concerned only with themselves and their own. It was a good business move to take the mark. That mark meant social acceptance, a climb up the corporate ladder, promotions, and more money. The goats had no time for the suffering Jewish remnant. In fact, there were glad to help the Beast attempt to eradicate this blight called Jews from planet Earth.

Depart from me, ye cursed

This is also a fulfillment of the Abrahamic Covenant of **Genesis 12:3**, as **Matthew 25:34** was. The verse continues with the phrase **and curse him that curseth thee.** Once again, history bears this out. Every nation that has gone against Israel has lost its influence in world affairs, if not its very place in the world. We have seen anti-Semitism in Biblical times by the Egyptians, the Assyrians, the Babylonians, the Persians, the Greeks and the Romans. Throughout world history, God has kept this promise. We have seen the results of anti-Semitism in places like the Spanish Inquisition; the Russian pogroms; the holocaust of Nazi Germany; the British Empire's failure to enforce the Balfour Declaration; Europe's forced emigration of the Jewish people. We could go on and on, but these few examples show that the Lord Jesus is serious about keeping His promise to bless those who bless Israel, and curse those who curse Israel. These goats are the final fulfillment of that prophecy and promise. God is not mocked. He says what He means, and He means what He says. The Judgment of God is coming to all those who reject His Son. **Micah 5:15; 2 Thessalonians 1:9**

Everlasting fire

Hell is a real, literal, geographic place. The Lord Jesus spoke twice as much about Hell as He did about Heaven. Some examples are found in **Matthew 5:22; Matthew 5:29; Matthew 8:12-21; Matthew 9:43; Matthew 23:33; Mark 9:43-48;** and **Luke 16:19-31**. Other New Testament teachings on hell as an eternal fire include **2 Peter 2:4; Jude 1:6; Revelation 20:11-15;** and **Revelation 21:8**. The entire reason He came was to warn man of this awful place called Hell. He died on a Cross for our sins so that we might not go to the place called Hell. He desires to save man. Notice that the Lord Jesus used the same term for hell as He did for eternal life. In **John 3:16**, the Lord Jesus calls being saved everlasting life. This tells us that as long as eternity with Christ will last, so will the fires of hell last for the lost. Hell is real, and it is no joking matter.

Prepared for the devil and his angels

Hell was built for Satan and his followers. **Revelation 20:10** It was NOT built for man. God never intended for man to go to Hell. It is God's desire for ALL men to be saved. **1 Timothy 2:4**

> For I was an hungred, and ye gave me no meat: I was thirsty, and ye gave me no drink:
> [Matthew 25:42]

Ye gave me no meat

While the sheep Gentiles were risking their lives and livelihoods by feeding the Jewish people during the Tribulation, the goat Gentiles were all to eager to jump on the bandwagon of the Beast and join in the worldwide persecution of the Lord Jesus' brethren. Believers of all ages are to take care of the Lord's people. **James 2:14-16**

> I was a stranger, and ye took me not in: naked, and ye clothed me not: sick, and in prison, and ye visited me not.
>
> [Matthew 25:43]

Ye visited me not

Notice that the Lord Jesus does not accuse the goat Gentiles of any direct persecution of His brethren. Their sin is merely a sin of neglect. It is not that these goat Gentiles actively joined in the Beast's persecution of the Jewish people, they were merely passive in their attitudes and actions. In other words, they did nothing. To do nothing is a damning sin. To do nothing with the Gospel will send a soul to hell. To neglect God's offer of salvation will land a person in hell for all eternity.

> Then shall they also answer him, saying, Lord, when saw we thee an hungred, or athirst, or a stranger, or naked, or sick, or in prison, and did

not minister unto thee?

[Matthew 25:44]

When saw we Thee

As the sheep were surprised by their invitation, the goats are shocked by their sentence. These goats bleat bitterly. They want to know when they saw the King, and treated Him is such a way. Sure, they hated the Jews, but if they had known the Gospel of the Kingdom were true, they never would have treated His people that way. It was the Jews they helped kill, not the King. That is their lame defense. However, like the sheep, their actions also show what is in their hearts.

> Then shall he answer them, saying, Verily I say unto you, Inasmuch as ye did *it* not to one of the least of these, ye did *it* not to me.
>
> **[Matthew 25:45]**

Ye did it not to Me

The goats despised the Lord Jesus in their hearts. They refused to believe in some fairy tale of a Coming Messiah-King. They hated Him and His brethren as well. They rejected the Gospel of the Kingdom. They were not heinous sinners, after all. They may have never committed murder, theft, or adultery. The sin they are guilty of is not accepting the Gospel. Unfortunately, they were guilty of the

ONLY sin that will condemn a soul to hell for all eternity. They were not believers. It was simply a sin of omission. EVERY soul in Hell for eternity will be there because of a sin of omission. They will NOT have accepted the Lord Jesus Christ as Saviour. **John 3:18**

> And these shall go away into everlasting punishment: but the righteous into life eternal.
>
> [**Matthew 25:46**]

Everlasting punishment: but the righteous into life eternal

Many cults and false religions do not believe in the eternality of hell. They teach that there is a time of suffering, but the soul will burn up after a time of paying for their sins, and be consigned to oblivion. However, that is not the teaching of Scripture. This verse teaches exactly the opposite. The Greek word for both **everlasting** and **eternal** in this verse is the SAME Greek word *aionios*. It means exactly what it is translated as. It means "everlasting," "eternal," "never-ending," and "without end." In other words, this verse teaches that everlasting punishment will continue just as long as eternal life will. As long as there is a Heaven, there will be a Hell. It is the same Greek word that is used as a modifier for both punishment and life. The truth is that every person who was ever born will live forever. All of us have eternal life because we are made in the image of God, and He is eternal life. The only question is where will you be spending that eternal life. In Heaven, or in Hell? The choice is yours.

Our Lord's Olivet Discourse teaches us many things. A few points to remember are 1) God is not through with the Nation of Israel. There is a common false teaching going around today that the Church has replaced Israel in the program and plan of God. This is NOT Scriptural. Our Lord's sermon on the Mount of Olives shows the exact opposite, as does **Romans 9-11**. 2) The Old Testament prophecies and promises of the Millennial Kingdom will be fulfilled. God always keeps His Word. 3) God is going to judge the world. This is the opposite of the humanistic teaching that if there is a loving God, he will not send anybody to Hell. 4) The Church is not to be looking for signs, we are to be looking for a Saviour. We are not looking for a sign, we are listening for a sound—the sound of a trumpet. **1 Thessalonians 4:16** 5) Jesus IS coming again. The question is will YOU be ready?

The only way to be ready is to be a believer. First you must confess you are a sinner. The Word of God tells us that ALL people have sinned. **Romans 3:23** All sinners deserve hell, because eternal separation from God is the wage of sin. **Romans 6:23** But God loves man, and wants to spend eternity with him. Because there is nothing we could do to earn God's salvation, HE had to do something. He did. He sent His Only-Begotten Son to save mankind from his sin. **John 3:16** All it takes to become a believer is to admit your sin, repent of (or turn from) your sin, accept the salvation that God offers through His Son's Death on the Cross, believe in your heart that God raised Him from the dead, and confess with your mouth that you believe this in your heart. **Romans 10:9-10** God has promised NEVER to turn away anybody who will come to Him. **Romans 10:13; John 6:37** Once you have made that decision, He promises to keep you until the end. **John 5:24** Why not come to salvation in Jesus today? Eternity will fill in the rest of the story.

APPENDIX

The Olivet Discourse

A compiled aggregate of the verses that make up the Lord Jesus' Olivet Discourse from the Four Gospels

Matthew 24:1 And Jesus went out, and departed from the temple:

Mark 13:1 ...one of his disciples saith unto him, Master, see what manner of stones and what buildings *are here*!

Matthew 24:1 ...and his disciples came to *him* for to shew him the buildings of the temple.

Luke 21:5 And as some spake of the temple, how it was adorned with goodly stones and gifts,

Matthew 24:2 And Jesus said unto them, See ye not all these things? ...

Mark 13:2 ...Seest thou these great buildings?

Matthew 24:2 ...verily I say unto you, There shall not be left here one stone upon another, that shall not be thrown down.

Matthew 24:3 And as he sat upon the mount of Olives, the disciples...

Mark 13:3 ...Peter and James and John and Andrew asked him privately,...

Matthew 24:3 ...saying, Tell us, when shall these things be? and what *shall be* the sign of thy coming, and of the end of the world?

Matthew 24:4 And Jesus answered and said unto them, Take heed that no man deceive you.

Matthew 24:5 For many shall come in my name, saying, I am Christ;...

Luke 21:8 ...and the time draweth near:...

Matthew 24:5 ...and shall deceive many.

Luke 21:8 ...go ye not therefore after them.

Matthew 24:6 And ye shall hear of wars and rumours of wars: see that ye be not troubled: for all *these things* must come to pass, but the end is not yet.

Matthew 24:7 For nation shall rise against nation, and kingdom against kingdom: and there shall be famines, and pestilences, and earthquakes, in divers places.

Luke 21:11 ...and fearful sights and great signs shall there be from heaven.

Matthew 24:8 All these *are* the beginning of sorrows.

Matthew 24:9 Then shall they deliver you up to be afflicted,...

Mark 13:9 ...for they shall deliver you up to councils; and in the synagogues ye shall be beaten: and ye shall be brought before rulers and kings for my sake, for a testimony against them...

Matthew 24:9 ...and shall kill you: and ye shall be hated of all nations for my name's sake.

Mark 13:11 But when they shall lead you, and deliver you up, take no thought beforehand what ye shall speak, neither do ye premeditate: but whatsoever shall be given you in that hour, that speak ye: for it is not ye that speak, but the Holy Ghost.

Luke 21:13 And it shall turn to you for a testimony.

Luke 21:14 Settle *it* therefore in your hearts, not to meditate before what ye shall answer:

Luke 21:15 For I will give you a mouth and wisdom, which all your adversaries shall not be able to gainsay nor resist.

Luke 21:16 And ye shall be betrayed both by parents, and brethren, and kinsfolks, and friends; ...

Mark 13:12 Now the brother shall betray the brother to death, and the father the son; and children shall rise up against *their* parents, ...

Luke 21:16 ... and *some* of you shall they cause to be put to death.

Luke 21:17 And ye shall be hated of all *men* for my name's sake.

Luke 21:18 But there shall not an hair of your head perish.

Luke 21:19 In your patience possess ye your souls.

Mark 13:12 Now the brother shall betray the brother to death, and the father the son; and children shall rise up against *their* parents, and shall cause them to be put to death.

Matthew 24:10 And then shall many be offended, and shall betray one another, and shall hate one another.

Matthew 24:11 And many false prophets shall

rise, and shall deceive many.

Matthew 24:12 And because iniquity shall abound, the love of many shall wax cold.

Matthew 24:13 But he that shall endure unto the end, the same shall be saved.

Luke 21:20 And when ye shall see Jerusalem compassed with armies, then know that the desolation thereof is nigh.

Luke 21:21 Then let them which are in Judaea flee to the mountains; and let them which are in the midst of it depart out; and let not them that are in the countries enter thereinto.

Luke 21:22 For these be the days of vengeance, that all things which are written may be fulfilled.

Luke 21:23 But woe unto them that are with child, and to them that give suck, in those days! for there shall be great distress in the land, and wrath upon this people.

Luke 21:24 And they shall fall by the edge of the sword, and shall be led away captive into all nations: and Jerusalem shall be trodden down of the Gentiles, until the times of the Gentiles be fulfilled.

Matthew 24:14 And this gospel of the kingdom

shall be preached in all the world for a witness unto all nations; and then shall the end come.

Matthew 24:15 When ye therefore shall see the abomination of desolation, spoken of by Daniel the prophet, stand in the holy place, (whoso readeth, let him understand:)

Matthew 24:16 Then let them which be in Judaea flee into the mountains:

Matthew 24:17 Let him which is on the housetop not come down to take any thing out of his house:

Mark 13:15 ...neither enter *therein*, to take any thing out of his house:

Matthew 24:18 Neither let him which is in the field return back to take his clothes.

Luke 17:32 Remember Lot's wife.

Luke 17:33 Whosoever shall seek to save his life shall lose it; and whosoever shall lose his life shall preserve it.

Matthew 24:19 And woe unto them that are with child, and to them that give suck in those days!

Matthew 24:20 But pray ye that your flight be not in the winter, neither on the sabbath day:

Matthew 24:21 For then shall be great tribulation, such as was not since the beginning of the world...

Mark 13:19 ...from the beginning of the creation which God created...

Matthew 24:21 ...to this time, no, nor ever shall be.

Matthew 24:22 And except those days should be shortened, there should no flesh be saved: but for the elect's sake those days shall be shortened.

Matthew 24:23 Then if any man shall say unto you, Lo, here *is* Christ, or there; believe *it* not.

Matthew 24:24 For there shall arise false Christs, and false prophets, and shall shew great signs and wonders; insomuch that, if *it were* possible, they shall deceive the very elect.

Mark 13:23 But take ye heed:...

Matthew 24:25 Behold, I have told you before.

Matthew 24:26 Wherefore if they shall say unto you, Behold, he is in the desert; go not forth: behold, *he is* in the secret chambers; believe *it* not.

Luke 17:23 ...go not after *them*, nor follow *them*.

Matthew 24:27 For as the lightning cometh out of the east, and shineth even unto the west; so shall also the coming of the Son of man be.

Matthew 24:28 For wheresoever the carcase is, there will the eagles be gathered together.

Luke 21:25 And there shall be signs in the sun, and in the moon, and in the stars; and upon the earth distress of nations, with perplexity; the sea and the waves roaring;

Matthew 24:29 Immediately after the tribulation of those days shall the sun be darkened, and the moon shall not give her light, and the stars shall fall from heaven, and the powers of the heavens shall be shaken:

Luke 21:26 Men's hearts failing them for fear, and for looking after those things which are coming on the earth:...

Matthew 24:30 And then shall appear the sign of the Son of man in heaven: and then shall all the tribes of the earth mourn, and they shall see the Son of man coming in the clouds of heaven with power and great glory.

Matthew 24:31 And he shall send his angels with a great sound of a trumpet, and they shall gather together his elect from the four winds, from one end of heaven to the other.

Matthew 24:32 Now learn a parable of the fig tree; ...

Luke 21:29 ...and all the trees...

Matthew 24:32 ...When his branch is yet tender, and putteth forth leaves, ye know that summer *is* nigh:

Matthew 24:33 So likewise ye, when ye shall see all these things, know that it is near, ...

Luke 21:31 ...that the kingdom of God is nigh at hand...

Matthew 24:33 ...*even* at the doors.

Matthew 24:34 Verily I say unto you, This generation shall not pass, till all these things be fulfilled.

Luke 21:28 And when these things begin to come to pass, then look up, and lift up your heads; for your redemption draweth nigh.

Matthew 24:35 Heaven and earth shall pass away, but my words shall not pass away.

Matthew 24:36 But of that day and hour knoweth no *man*, no, not the angels of heaven, ...

Mark 13:32 …neither the Son…

Matthew 24:35 …but my Father only.

Matthew 24:37 But as the days of Noe *were*, so shall also the coming of the Son of man be.

Matthew 24:38 For as in the days that were before the flood they were eating and drinking, marrying and giving in marriage, until the day that Noe entered into the ark,

Matthew 24:39 And knew not until the flood came, and took them all away; so shall also the coming of the Son of man be.

Luke 17:28 Likewise also as it was in the days of Lot; they did eat, they drank, they bought, they sold, they planted, they builded;

Luke 17:29 But the same day that Lot went out of Sodom it rained fire and brimstone from heaven, and destroyed *them* all.

Luke 17:30 Even thus shall it be in the day when the Son of man is revealed.

Matthew 24:40 Then shall two be in the field; the one shall be taken, and the other left.

Luke 17:34 I tell you, in that night there shall be two *men* in one bed; the one shall be taken, and the other shall be left.

Matthew 24:41 Two *women shall be* grinding at the mill; the one shall be taken, and the other left.

Luke 17:37 And they answered and said unto him, Where, Lord? And he said unto them, Wheresoever the body *is*, thither will the eagles be gathered together.

Luke 21:34 And take heed to yourselves, lest at any time your hearts be overcharged with surfeiting, and drunkenness, and cares of this life, and *so* that day come upon you unawares.

Luke 21:35 For as a snare shall it come on all them that dwell on the face of the whole earth.

Matthew 24:42 Watch therefore: for ye know not what hour your Lord doth come.

Luke 21:36 Watch ye therefore, and pray always, that ye may be accounted worthy to escape all these things that shall come to pass, and to stand before the Son of man.

Mark 13:34 *For the Son of man is* as a man taking a far journey, who left his house, and gave authority to his servants, and to every man his work, and commanded the porter to watch.

Mark 13:35 Watch ye therefore: for ye know not when the master of the house cometh, at even, or at midnight, or at the cockcrowing, or in the morning:

Mark 13:36 Lest coming suddenly he find you sleeping.

Mark 13:37 And what I say unto you I say unto all, Watch.

Matthew 24:43 But know this, that if the good-man of the house had known in what watch the thief would come, he would have watched, and would not have suffered his house to be broken up.

Matthew 24:44 Therefore be ye also ready: for in such an hour as ye think not the Son of man cometh.

Matthew 24:45 Who then is a faithful and wise servant, whom his lord hath made ruler over his household, to give them meat in due season?

Matthew 24:46 Blessed *is* that servant, whom his lord when he cometh shall find so doing.

Matthew 24:47 Verily I say unto you, That he shall make him ruler over all his goods.

Matthew 24:48 But and if that evil servant shall

say in his heart, My lord delayeth his coming;

Matthew 24:49 And shall begin to smite *his* fellowservants, and to eat and drink with the drunken;

Matthew 24:50 The lord of that servant shall come in a day when he looketh not for *him*, and in an hour that he is not aware of,

Matthew 24:51 And shall cut him asunder, and appoint *him* his portion with the hypocrites: there shall be weeping and gnashing of teeth.

Matthew 25:1 Then shall the kingdom of heaven be likened unto ten virgins, which took their lamps, and went forth to meet the bridegroom.

Matthew 25:2 And five of them were wise, and five *were* foolish.

Matthew 25:3 They that *were* foolish took their lamps, and took no oil with them:

Matthew 25:4 But the wise took oil in their vessels with their lamps.

Matthew 25:5 While the bridegroom tarried, they all slumbered and slept.

Matthew 25:6 And at midnight there was a cry made, Behold, the bridegroom cometh; go ye out to meet him.

Matthew 25:7 Then all those virgins arose, and trimmed their lamps.

Matthew 25:8 And the foolish said unto the wise, Give us of your oil; for our lamps are gone out.

Matthew 25:9 But the wise answered, saying, *Not so*; lest there be not enough for us and you: but go ye rather to them that sell, and buy for yourselves.

Matthew 25:10 And while they went to buy, the bridegroom came; and they that were ready went in with him to the marriage: and the door was shut.

Matthew 25:11 Afterward came also the other virgins, saying, Lord, Lord, open to us.

Matthew 25:12 But he answered and said, Verily I say unto you, I know you not.

Matthew 25:13 Watch therefore, for ye know neither the day nor the hour wherein the Son of man cometh.

Matthew 25:14 For *the kingdom of heaven is* as a man travelling into a far country, *who* called his own servants, and delivered unto them his goods.

Matthew 25:15 And unto one he gave five talents, to another two, and to another one; to every man according to his several ability; and straightway took his journey.

Matthew 25:16 Then he that had received the five talents went and traded with the same, and made *them* other five talents.

Matthew 25:17 And likewise he that *had received* two, he also gained other two.

Matthew 25:18 But he that had received one went and digged in the earth, and hid his lord's money.

Matthew 25:19 After a long time the lord of those servants cometh, and reckoneth with them.

Matthew 25:20 And so he that had received five talents came and brought other five talents, saying, Lord, thou deliveredst unto me five talents: behold, I have gained beside them five talents more.

Matthew 25:21 His lord said unto him, Well done, *thou* good and faithful servant: thou hast been faithful over a few things, I will make thee ruler over many things: enter thou into the joy of thy lord.

Matthew 25:22 He also that had received two talents came and said, Lord, thou deliveredst unto me two talents: behold, I have gained two other talents beside them.

Matthew 25:23 His lord said unto him, Well done, good and faithful servant; thou hast been faithful over a few things, I will make thee ruler over many things: enter thou into the joy of thy lord.

Matthew 25:24 Then he which had received the one talent came and said, Lord, I knew thee that thou art an hard man, reaping where thou hast not sown, and gathering where thou hast not strawed:

Matthew 25:25 And I was afraid, and went and hid thy talent in the earth: lo, *there* thou hast *that is* thine.

Matthew 25:26 His lord answered and said unto him, *Thou* wicked and slothful servant, thou knewest that I reap where I sowed not, and gather where I have not strawed:

Matthew 25:27 Thou oughtest therefore to have put my money to the exchangers, and *then* at my coming I should have received mine own with usury.

Matthew 25:28 Take therefore the talent from him, and give *it* unto him which hath ten talents.

Matthew 25:29 For unto every one that hath shall be given, and he shall have abundance: but from him that hath not shall be taken away even that which he hath.

Matthew 25:30 And cast ye the unprofitable servant into outer darkness: there shall be weeping and gnashing of teeth.

Matthew 25:31 When the Son of man shall come in his glory, and all the holy angels with him, then shall he sit upon the throne of his glory:

Matthew 25:32 And before him shall be gathered all nations: and he shall separate them one from another, as a shepherd divideth *his* sheep from the goats:

Matthew 25:33 And he shall set the sheep on his right hand, but the goats on the left.

Matthew 25:34 Then shall the King say unto them on his right hand, Come, ye blessed of my Father, inherit the kingdom prepared for you from the foundation of the world:

Matthew 25:35 For I was an hungred, and ye gave me meat: I was thirsty, and ye gave me drink: I was a stranger, and ye took me in:

Matthew 25:36 Naked, and ye clothed me: I was sick, and ye visited me: I was in prison, and ye came unto me.

Matthew 25:37 Then shall the righteous answer him, saying, Lord, when saw we thee an hungred, and fed *thee*? or thirsty, and gave thee drink?

Matthew 25:38 When saw we thee a stranger, and took thee in? or naked, and clothed *thee*?

Matthew 25:39 Or when saw we thee sick, or in prison, and came unto thee?

Matthew 25:40 And the King shall answer and say unto them, Verily I say unto you, Inasmuch as ye have done *it* unto one of the least of these my brethren, ye have done *it* unto me.

Matthew 25:41 Then shall he say also unto them on the left hand, Depart from me, ye cursed, into everlasting fire, prepared for the devil and his angels:

Matthew 25:42 For I was an hungred, and ye gave me no meat: I was thirsty, and ye gave me no drink:

Matthew 25:43 I was a stranger, and ye took me not in: naked, and ye clothed me not: sick, and in prison, and ye visited me not.

Matthew 25:44 Then shall they also answer him, saying, Lord, when saw we thee an hungred, or athirst, or a stranger, or naked, or sick, or in prison, and did not minister unto thee?

Matthew 25:45 Then shall he answer them, saying, Verily I say unto you, Inasmuch as ye did *it* not to one of the least of these, ye did *it* not to me.

Matthew 25:46 And these shall go away into everlasting punishment: but the righteous into life eternal.

Bibliography

Anstey, Bruce, The Olivet Discourse: Matthew 24-25. (Surrey, British Colombia: Christian Truth Publishing), 2006.

Armerding, Carl, The Olivet Discourse: An Exposition of Matthew 24 and 25. (Findlay, Ohio: Dunham Publishing Company), 1955.

Beirnes, William, Exposition of the Olivet Discourse. (Tequesta, Florida: The Midnight Cry), n.d.

Beasley-Murray, George R., Jesus and the Last Days: The Interpretation of the Olivet Discourse. (Peabody, Massachusetts: Hendrickson Publishers), 1993.

Bloomfield, Arthur E., Signs of His Coming: A Study of the Olivet Discourse. (Minneapolis, Minnesota: Bethany House Publishers), 1979.

Darby, John Nelson, Synopsis of the Books of the Bible: Volume 3 Matthew to John. (Sunbury, Pennsylvania: Believer's Bookshelf), 1992.

Falwell, Jerry, ed., King James Bible Commentary. (Nashville: Thomas Nelson Publishers), 1999.

Fruchtenbaum, Arnold G., <u>The Footsteps of the Messiah</u>. (Tustin, California: Ariel Ministries), 2004.

Gaebelein, Arno C., <u>The Olivet Discourse</u>. (Greenville, South Carolina: The Gospel Hour, Inc.), nd.

Gray, James M., <u>The Concise Bible Commentary</u>. (Peabody, Massachusetts: Hendrickson Publishers), 1999.

Greene, Oliver B., <u>The Gospel According to Matthew: Volumes V and VI</u>. (Greenville, South Carolina: The Gospel Hour, Inc.), 1975.

Hindson, Ed, <u>The End of the World Foretold by the Son of God</u>. (Colton, California: World Prophetic Ministry, Inc.), 2006.

Hindson, Edward and James Borland, <u>Matthew: The King is Coming</u>. (Chattanooga, Tennessee: AMG Publishers), 2006.

Hitchcock, Mark, <u>What Jesus Says About Earth's Final Days</u>. (Sisters, Oregon: Multnomah Publishers), 2003.

Hutchings, N.W., <u>Problem Prophetic Passages: Volume 1 The Olivet Discourse</u>. (Oklahoma City, Oklahoma: Hearthstone Publishing, Ltd.), 1991.

Ironside, H. A., <u>Matthew</u>. (Baltimore: Loizeaux Brothers, Inc.), 1994.

Jeremiah, David, <u>Until I Come</u>. (Nashville: Word Publishing), 1999.

Kelly, William, <u>The Lord's Prophecy on the Mount of Olives: Volume 1 of Three Prophetic Gems</u>. (Sunbury, Pennsylvania: Believers Bookshelf), 2007.

LaHaye, Tim and Ed Hindson, <u>The Popular Bible Prophecy Commentary</u>. (Eugene, Oregon: Harvest House Publishers), 2006.

Lieth, Norbert, <u>Hidden Signs in the Olivet Discourse</u>. (Columbia, South Carolina: The Olive Press), 2005.

MacArthur, John, <u>The Second Coming: Signs of Christ's Return and the End of the Age</u>. (Wheaton, Illinois: Crossway Books), 1999.

MacDonald, William, <u>Believer's Bible Commentary</u>. (Nashville: Thomas Nelson Publishers), 1995.

McGee, J. Vernon, <u>From the Top of the Mount of Olives on a Clear Day You Can See Forever</u>. (Pasadena, California: Thru the Bible Books), 1984.

McGee, J. Vernon, <u>Thru the Bible with J. Vernon McGee: Volume IV Matthew-Romans</u>. (Nashville: Thomas Nelson Publishers), 1983.

Pentecost, J. Dwight, Things To Come: A Study in Biblical Eschatology. (Grand Rapids, Michigan: Zondervan Publishing House), 1958.

Phillips, John, Exploring the Future: A Comprehensive Guide to Bible Prophecy. (Grand Rapids, Michigan: Kregel Publications), 2003.

Price, Walter K., Jesus' Prophetic Sermon: The Olivet Key to Israel, the Church, and the Nations. (Chicago: Moody Press), 1972.

Ruckman, Peter S., The Book of Matthew. (Pensacola, Florida: Pensacola Bible Institute), 1978.

Scofield, C.I., ed., The Scofield Study Bible. (New York: Oxford University Press), 1996.

Shelton, Bob, Prophecy in Context: A Look at the Olivet Discourse. (Greenville, SC: JourneyForth), 2008.

Sorenson, David, Understanding the Bible: Matthew through Luke. (Duluth, Minnesota: Northstar Ministries), 2005.

Stedman, Ray, What on Earth is Happening? What Jesus Said About the End of the Age. (Grand Rapids, Michigan: Discovery House Publishers), 2003.

Walvoord, John F., <u>Matthew: Thy Kingdom Come</u>. (Grand Rapids, Michigan: Kregel Publications), 1974.

Walvoord, John F., <u>The Prophecy Knowledge Handbook</u>. (Wheaton, Illinois: Victor Books), 1990.

Walvoord, John F. and Roy B. Zuck, eds., <u>The Bible Knowledge Commentary New Testament</u>. (Wheaton, Illinois: Victor Books), nd.

Wiersbe, Warren W., <u>The Bible Exposition Commentary New Testament: Volume 1</u>. (Colorado Springs, Colorado: Victor Books), 2001.

Willmington, Harold L., <u>The Outline Bible</u>. (Wheaton, Illinois: Tyndale House Publishers, Inc.), 1999.

Willmington, Harold L., <u>Willmington's Guide to the Bible</u>. (Carol Stream, Illinois: Tyndale House), 1984.

Zodhiates, Spiros, <u>Exegetical commentary on Matthew</u>. (Chattanooga, Tennessee: AMG Publishers), 2006.

CONTACT

Charlie Fouché
969 Baker Road SW
Dalton, GA 30720
e-mail: charliefouche@gmail.com

THE TWO O'CLOCK KILLER

A SHORT STORY BY

NIZ THOMAS

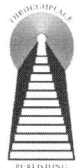